YOU CAN'T DO WHAT?

The Real Meaning of Your Salvation

❖

YOU CAN'T DO WHAT?

The Real Meaning of Your Salvation

Dr. Valerie K. Brown

Pastoral Comments by Bishop K. W. Brown
Presiding Prelate
Mount Global Fellowship of Churches

Spirit Filled Creations

YOU CAN'T DO WHAT?
The Real Meaning of Your Salvation
Published by Spirit Filled Creations
3509 Kids Court
Chesapeake, Virginia 23323
SpiritFilledCreations7@gmail.com

Unless otherwise indicated, all Scripture quotations are taken from the *Holy Bible*, New Living Translation, copyright © 1996. Used by permission of Tyndale House Publishers, Inc., Wheaton, Illinois 60189. All rights reserved.

Cover Design: Donnie Ramsey

International Standard Book Number: 978-0-9653696-3-3

First Edition

Printed in the United States of America

❖

DEDICATION & THANK YOU

I want to take this opportunity to thank the many people who have encouraged me, motivated me, and given me this opportunity to see this book in print. First, I want to thank the Holy Spirit, who I know, without a doubt guided me through this entire process. My prayer throughout this book is that God is pleased with the final product and it will enlighten and provide continued revelation to a Kingdom model of church and not religion.

Kim Walter Brown, Presiding Prelate of the Mount Global Fellowship of Churches, thank you for over twenty-five years of marriage. It has been through this journey as your wife, mother of your two children, and ministering beside you as the Executive Pastor of the Mount Global Fellowship of Churches that this book found its genesis. Without our stretching one another, challenging one another, and even disagreeing with one another, to dig and search for the Kingdom of God and not denominational traditions, neither one of us would have grown in our spiritual maturity and walk with God to be where we are today. I love you dearly for putting up with me always questioning, "Why, why, why we believe this and that" as if I was a two-year-old discovering Christianity for the first time. It is sad to say; however, that in many ways, I was.

Thank you to my children, James and Kimberly, and my daughter in love, Keshia, for providing much insight and wisdom for your ages. You helped me to wrestle with what the Bible says versus what man-made traditions say.

I love how you all love the Lord and desire to find your unique purpose in God's perfect will for your lives. I also love that you want your lives to be examples to other young adults. You too have gone through this journey with me to help shape young adult lives and the journey of the many dos and don'ts of living life as a saved young adult Christian.

To the Mount Global Fellowship of Churches, I love serving as your Executive Pastor. Thank you for being so supportive and generous. It is because of your having the heart to please God and a yearning for truth that I was compelled to answer many of the questions that I will discuss in this book.

And last but certainly not least, I want to thank my publisher, Monique Jewell Anderson. Monique was sent by God to help me push through this final phase of editing and encouraging me to share my personal stories so that everyone reading this book can see the struggle I have had and have overcome.

To my followers, a huge thank you, for allowing me space in your busy schedule to even read this book. This is my third book, and I already have the blueprint for a few more books to come. My prayer never changes for each of you. That prayer is that nothing I write or say distracts you from having a closer relationship with Jesus Christ, the Holy Spirit, and God our Father. I pray for new and fresh revelations that will enable you to draw closer to Him daily.

❖

❖❖ Table of Contents ❖❖

❖

❖❖ Table of Contents ❖❖
(continued)

❖❖ **INTRODUCTION** ❖❖

Have you ever wondered what the life of Jesus would look like if he walked the Earth today? Would we find him salsa dancing in a Miami nightclub, at a friend's house playing a card game, or even lounging on a hot sandy beach enjoying a frozen Margarita? Would we find Jesus laughing at a Broadway show, enjoying a beer and a chili hot dog at a basketball game, or otherwise simply enjoying life? And if we did, would we question whether Jesus was a saved Christian?

These are the questions that I have been asked to answer by many in the congregation that my husband and I pastor. I serve as the Executive Pastor of what started as a traditional Baptist church over one hundred years ago. When we began, the church had only seventy-five members but has now grown to over twelve thousand members with multiple locations. While I grew up in the traditional Baptist Church, like most young people, I strayed away during my college and post-college years. I was not what one would call a wild child, but I did indulge in college parties, drank alcoholic beverages, and naturally enjoyed living. Fast-forward a few years to when I met my husband who had just become a licensed minister of the gospel. His background was also from a traditional Baptist church with his father having also been a Baptist minister. My husband led a very simple life and did not believe in drinking alcoholic beverages, attending parties, dancing, playing cards, or any of the many activities that I thought were a natural part of growing up.

I remember when we were dating some of my college friends and I attended the CIAA basketball tournament. I asked him to join us and he did. After the game, we were hungry, so my friends suggested we eat. The restaurant we chose, like many restaurants, had a bar. He immediately said he did not want to go with us to eat at that particular restaurant because of the bar. We laughed because we thought for sure he must have been joking. What does a restaurant with a bar have to do with the fact that we were going to eat? He insisted on not going. At that point in our relationship, we were not discussing marriage, and I wanted to hang out, so we said goodnight and I went to eat with my friends. At the time, I did not put too much emphasis on this exchange or his beliefs; however, I could not help but pause momentarily and ask myself, *was I being a heathen by going to a restaurant that had a bar?* While I was not in church every Sunday, I had been baptized and believed I was saved and living a life (while not perfect) acceptable to being called a saved Christian.

As our relationship became serious and we began to talk about marriage, my husband (to be) and I had many conversations regarding our beliefs about our future together. We shared our thoughts about issues we considered deal-breakers. Since I had gone down the marriage aisle once before, I was committed to avoiding divorce. He had no problem with it as he believed when two people want to be married and love each other they can work through any problems. He asked me, however, to commit to refraining from drinking any alcoholic beverages. No wine? Wow! I was far from an alcoholic, but I did enjoy drinking a glass or two of wine with dinner and socially when out with friends. But because I loved him and wanted to marry him (and he put a ring on it), I agreed to his request from that day forward. That was over twenty-five years ago, and I have held to my word and my commitment to him. My friends could not believe it and always questioned the rationale and purpose as none of them could find support for my stance in the Bible. This was the beginning of a long journey in our marriage of discovery about his beliefs, my beliefs, and what the Bible says about a lot of different topics regarding things Christians can and cannot do.

When we married, we moved into the home I was already living in. Before marrying him, one of my neighbors and I would regularly play a card game called, Bid Whist. Never in a thousand years, would I think he would also object to playing this game, mainly since there is no money or gambling associated with it. In fact, the game is filled with strategy and fun and is no different than the game of Scrabble or chess. However, because cards were involved his belief was that I could not play this particular game. His view also extended to games with dice. My beliefs were on the opposite spectrum. While growing up, my family played many games with and without dice to include Monopoly, Clue, chess, as well as various cards games. My childhood home was filled with laughter and fun. Then I found myself being told by my husband that I was not a saved Christian if I played games with dice. Moreover, many of the pastors we associated with during this season shared the same belief as my husband. However, none of them could give me scripture for their belief. Their response was, "Baptist Christians do not do these things." I was confused. I did not understand.

The traditional Baptist church is known for its strict standards when it comes to what the lifestyle of a saved Christian should resemble. I dare say, many of the traditional Baptist members would quickly answer the questions I posed at the beginning of this book with "No way, Jesus would never drink an alcoholic beverage, be seen in a nightclub, dance, or play any card game." Back then, I also could not have responded to any of those questions posed from a biblical perspective because, the reality was, I did not know the Bible well enough to do so. I had not read it from front to back cover. I had not studied it for answers. I was like so many other saved Christians who came to church and opened the Bible when the preacher read a scripture for his sermon topic and then closed the Bible, not to open it again until perhaps Wednesday night Bible Study or the next Sunday's sermon. However, as our congregation grew and more millennials began to unite with our church, they were not as willing as baby boomers to accept answers, without question, by the pastor; but instead asked us, their shepherds, to show them in the Bible where the answer to these questions were. The difference with me is I have never been able to accept just any old thing. I needed specific answers as well. So, I found myself joining in on their quest because I was no longer willing to accept the *Baptist Christians do or don't do* party line. I wanted to know what the Bible said I can and cannot do, and I wanted answers that were rooted in biblical scripture; not man-made traditions or ideals. As I began my study, I found scriptures that had been used for years to justify a particular stance or belief; however, I also found many of these scriptures were used out of context. Most surprisingly, I found more scriptures that painted a clearer picture and understanding of the message of what a saved Christian life should emulate. Looking back, I honestly believe it was the Holy Spirit urging me to get to know the Bible, not just so I could have some fun, but because there was going to be a call on my life that I would have to answer in order to help educate the Body of Christ.

What has come to be so amazing is that it is not only the Baptist Christians who are asking these questions but unsaved people as well. I have had unsaved people tell me the reason they do not want to become saved is that they have been told, "You cannot have any more fun once you accept Jesus Christ as your Savior." Initially, as much as I wanted to tell them they were wrong, deep down, I understood what they were saying because I felt I could no longer hang out with my friends because they still drank alcoholic beverages. My friends still had parties and danced. My friends still played Bid Whist, but unfortunately these environments were frowned upon for a saved Baptist First Lady like me.

My *fun* was gone.

The reality is, questions concerning the Christian lifestyle are not new and have been asked by every generation, yet the answers still elude the Body of Christ. The reasons for this perhaps lies in the fact that the questions are not easily answered because for every scripture used, there is always someone to offer a different interpretation of that scripture to support whichever side of the argument that's preferred. Therefore, it is no surprise that the Body of Christ is bi-polar. Leaders within the church cannot agree on what a scripture is saying, so the laity often decides for themselves what they believe a saved Christian lifestyle should entail.

All of this and more has lead to the call on my life and this book. I believe I have had these experiences and discussions with my husband, our congregational members, and my unsaved friends so I would be challenged to go and find scriptures that would open a fresh and necessary new dialogue. Topics that have been answered or ignored and considered taboo from every perspective, except the Biblical one, need an unbiased revisit. I am by no means saying that there is not room for my positions to be challenged. However, what I have done is thrown out religion and denominational beliefs (which I cover in greater detail later in this book), and taken a fresh look at the Bible. I have asked the Holy Spirit to guide and direct me by giving me a revelation to be shared by all who are struggling to find these answers. Somewhere is the truth we are all searching for and one thing is for certain; the Bible has not been written to drive away the unsaved. The intent of the Bible was not written for people to live sad and boring lives. The Bible exists so that we would have a guide, a reference to how we should be living as Christians and how Jesus lived while here on Earth.

I am now a licensed minister of the gospel operating in the five-fold ministry with the gift of teaching. Bishop and I have been at the same church for over twenty-five years. I have served as the Executive Pastor for the last seventeen years because it took the first eight years for the church and my husband to accept the fact that a Baptist First Lady can do more than sit on the second pew and chair the hospitality committee. I hold an undergraduate degree in Accounting from Virginia State University, a Virginia CPA (1980 inactive), and a Doctorate of Management Degree from The Weatherhead School of Business, Case Western Reserve University. I have public accounting experience with Arthur Anderson and Co (Washington DC) and other corporate America companies, as well as, having had my own CPA firm for over fifteen years. I have also taught in the School of Business at Norfolk State University and the M. Div. program at The Samuel D. Proctor, School of Theology, at Virginia Union University. I shared all of my educational and work experiences to say that I love teaching. I believe God allowed my vast educational pursuits so that I could operate efficiently in the office as Executive Pastor and use these experiences to share wisdom with those whom I am blessed to influence. As you can attest to, I am not the Executive Pastor because I am the Pastor's wife. I like to say, "Yes, I am qualified to operate as the Executive Pastor, and the bonus is I get to sleep with the boss, and it's okay."

Let's take this journey together as we explore the scriptures that I believe have been inspired by the Holy Spirit to help us separate man-made traditions from biblical scripture. It is my desire to help illuminate the lifestyle God has for all of us to live as saved Christians. I believe this lifestyle is a life filled with laughter, enjoyment, and fun!

Elder Valerie

CHAPTER ONE

The Real Meaning of Your Salvation

T
he real meaning of your salvation is important because the Christian lifestyle and being saved have been confused and interchanged. To help restore our confidence in what is acceptable and unacceptable behavior for a Christian, we must first be able to say that we are Christians that have accepted Jesus as our Lord and Savior according to the teachings of Romans 10 verses 9-10. It reads, *"For if you confess with your mouth that Jesus is Lord and believe in your heart that God raised him from the dead, you will be saved. For it is by believing in your heart that you are made right with God, and it is by confessing with your mouth that you are saved."*

Many Christians were taught accepting Christ begins and ends with repeating the sinner's prayer, or walking down a church aisle one Sunday morning and shaking the Pastor's hand, or being baptized, or some combination of the above. Conversely, many Christians are now asking the question, "Isn't there more to my salvation than going to Heaven?" My answer to this issue is, "Absolutely!"

Our understanding of the connection between our behavior and receiving the gift of salvation is vital. It is

1

essential because part of the problem is that some are professing to be Christians but their lifestyles leave one to question whether their salvation is real. This has led to the question of what is appropriate behavior. However, before we even begin to explore what is appropriate behavior we have to be able *first* to determine who has actually been saved and is a Christian. So, that we watch *their* behavior and not the behavior of someone claiming to be a saved Christian but are not. Hence, the lifestyle of the latter is not subject to our scrutiny because they are not the example we should follow or address. Mathew 7:20 reminds us, *"Yes, the way to identify a tree or a person is by the kind of fruit that is produced."* That means if we watch an individual long enough their actions and behavior (fruit) will show us who they really are...not what they simply say they are. Being able to make this distinction will go a long way in eliminating a discussion on behaviors attributable to each individual. We will explore this determination as we delve further into this debate because the focus of this book is to center solely on the behavior of those who have legitimately been saved and who are trying desperately to live for Jesus Christ.

The confession with our mouths and the believing in our hearts, as recorded in Romans 10:9, is the scriptural foundation for our doubtless salvation. In Romans 12:1-3, Paul tells us that we are reborn in Christ Jesus with a renewing of our minds. Our focus in life should change and no longer be in the worldly pursuits of materialism and self-gratification, but on growing closer to Jesus each day.

For far too long Christians have quoted the scriptures mentioned above without sincerely taking the time to study their real and deeper meanings to be able to apply them to their daily living. Christians have been taught, directly or indirectly, that these scriptures somehow bind us to live an unexciting life of going to work and reading our bibles daily as our sole source of entertainment. Most believers envision Christian fun as getting together to dialogue about biblical passages, planning choir anniversaries, or similar activities. It is inconceivable that a truly saved Christian would enjoy going to the movies, bowling, playing cards, (or board games,) and laughing in church. This might sound crazy, but it is a daily reality for lots of Christians. What makes this even more crucial is the fact that many Unbelievers have this false imagery of Christianity too, which causes many of them to cite this dull life as the reason to not wanting to become a Christian. I have lost count the many times over the years that I have heard, "Christians are so boring and can't have any fun." Numerous Christians are sitting in church pews

Sunday after Sunday believing they should have drab and mundane lives. This is why many Christians are totally confused. Christians want to have fun. They want to laugh and enjoy life. They don't want to feel as though they are hiding anything from anyone. They are screaming for help and clarity in this area of their Christian walk.

Unfortunately, believers lack knowledge of biblical teachings of acceptable Christian behavior. Instead, their understanding is based on generations of traditions, examples, and false teachings. Their inner man (spirit) is in turmoil because they aspire to be holy, yet they still desire to have fun at the same time. Spending relaxed time and having fun with family and friends, usually leads to a night of internal struggle. This gives birth to attending church on Sunday feeling as though they must wear a holiness mask. The church has raised a generation of people who know how to do church on Sunday but who don't know how to live an authentic faith life.

The focus of Jesus' ministry was in teaching us how to live our lives daily to please God, the Father. Both the Old and New Testament spend the majority of the text teaching about Monday thru Saturday living; not just how to worship on the Sabbath. Why then do we think that putting on our sanctified masks in the church has fooled God into believing that our lives are holy? Who are we trying to trick? Are we deceiving our pastors? Are we trying to con our fellow Christian brothers and sisters? The scriptures say God knows our hearts. In fact, God knows everything. So who are we fooling with our masks? Better yet, whom are we trying to please by not having fun and laughing?

To think that whatever you do on Monday through Saturday can be erased or ignored by God by what you do on Sunday, then you need to think again. For if on Sunday you put on a holiness mask, sing a few praise songs, weep and cry, ask God for forgiveness, then start all over again doing what you want and living however you choose on Monday, then perhaps the saddest realization is that you are only fooling yourselves. Read Galatians 6:7, *"Do not be deceived. God is not mocked."* I encourage you to take off the mask and start being holy throughout the week. If being holy every day is too difficult or you think you cannot have fun while living holy, I ask you to reconsider. It may not be as much of a struggle as you think or have been told. Merriam-Webster's dictionary defines holy as "Exalted or worthy of complete devotion; goodness, righteousness; having a divine quality, or morally good." While I have searched other books for the definition of holy, I noticed that none defined it with terms such as long dresses, no make-up, no drinking alcoholic beverages, no laughing, or having no fun. So needless to say, I question those who try to define holy by any of these terms. Now is the time that the proven, mature believers in Christ read and study the Bible. You must know for yourselves what it says you can and cannot do.

Living the life of a saved Christian is not as difficult as we Christians sometimes make it out to be. Like the Pharisees of the Old Testament, we complicate the Word of God by attempting to be deep or profound in our interpretation of God's Word. We raise questions to issues about Christianity that can be found by easily going to the Bible and studying it. I believe we address some subjects, however, to get a discussion going that may result in an answer we want to hear from others (their interpretation) and not what God had intended the answer to be. This somehow validates and justifies our behavior, even though deep within our hearts we know our actions do not square up with the Word of God.

One such issue commonly addressed by Christians is, "Do we tithe on our gross or net income or do we have to tithe at all?" There have been more arguments and discussions over this question that God surely cannot be satisfied with us debating it. While I have not been able to search every translation and version of the Bible (I use the New Living Translation) I have yet to find either "gross" or "net," in any of the scriptures on tithing. So why are we debating about which word, gross or net, is the correct word? In Deuteronomy 14:22, God says, *give a tithe or ten percent of your income.* Most pastors I know would be thrilled if their members readily tithed on the net, let alone on gross. But these types of discussions are designed by Satan to give some Christians an excuse for not tithing. I've heard some Christians say, "I can't get a straight answer on how to tithe, so I just give what I think is right." Look at what we are doing to the body of Christ by entertaining these discussions. Even the Apostle Paul had to remind us of this fact in Second Timothy 2:14 where we find, *"Remind everyone about these things, and command them in God's presence to stop fighting over words. Such arguments are useless, and they can ruin those who hear them."*

So why are we fighting over words? Words are important. We rely on them to convey our messages one to another. But how many times have we had to apologize to someone because we listened intently to the choice of words and not to the essence of what they were trying to say? Therefore, we were misunderstood, and the person did not hear what we were attempting to communicate. We immediately had to respond with, "That's not what I meant," only to hear them respond with, "That's what you said."

Therefore, instead of fighting over words, we should be looking to God to reveal to us the understanding behind the words. (Colossians 1:9)

This brings us to yet another word that has been the subject of many a debate, and that word is salvation.

As I have studied the Bible and matured in doing so, I have realized that salvation is a gift from God and there is no amount of works that can earn us salvation. But do we really understand what it *means* to be saved? What must we *do* to be saved? Do we know what salvation *gives* us? Do we know how to *receive* it?

One would be surprised if there were a Christian anywhere who could not answer the common question, "What must I do to be saved?" As well as quote Romans 10:9, *"For if you confess with your mouth that Jesus is Lord and believe in your heart that God raised him from the dead, you will be saved."*

This is not a debatable scripture. If you are a Christian and if you believe the Word of God, you know that to be saved, to fully receive salvation, all you need to do is:

- ✓ ➢ Open your mouth and confess that Jesus is Lord; and,

- ✓ ➢ Believe in your heart that God raised his only Son, Jesus, from the dead.

It sounds so simple, and it is that simple. But as Christians, we must be sure we understand the meaning, message, and intent that God had in communicating these words to us in scripture. Using a word is not enough. We must also acknowledge our understanding of the meaning of the wording through our actions. Our actions require a simple two-step process.

> ➢ Step one is a mental mindset of comprehending the meanings of the words.
>
> ➢ Step two is an acknowledgment of our understanding through our actions.

For example, a husband tells his wife, "I love you girl." That's step one. She hears him because he opens his mouth and confesses his love to her. But how often have you witnessed a woman say, "He says he loves me, but he never shows me that he really loves me." Wives want their husbands to show them through their actions and by the things they do for them to say, "I love you." It is then, and only then, when step one and two is done that wives whole-heartedly believe their husbands love them.

Our goal as Christians should be to say to God, "I love you," and to show Him, daily through how we live our lives, that we really love Him. We do not want God to be like some wives, wondering if we really love Him because our mouths say one thing and our actions are saying another.

Have you ever asked this question about your salvation? "What am I saved from?" Maybe as a Christian, you already know this answer as it relates to Romans 10:9, but to ensure that everyone reading this book is on the same page, you and I will explore the answer a little further.

Let's look at John 3:16-17: *"For God so loved the world that he gave his only Son, so that everyone who believes in him will not perish but have eternal life. God did not send his Son into the world to condemn it, but to save it."*

It has always been God's intentional plan that humanity would have eternal life in Him. God's desire was that after a man had lived in his human vessel (his fleshly body), his natural death would not be unto a spiritual death. That is, man-kind would awake on that great day when we who have died under salvation would once again be able to rise and live eternally with our Heavenly Father. In simple terms, those who have confessed and believed, according to Romans 10:9, will be able to live again (in our spiritual bodies) in heaven with our Creator and Father, the Lord God.

So again, from what are we saved? We are saved from perishing; a life of eternal death and destruction in Hell. We know that Hell is real, that Satan rules it, and all who fail to believe in God will face judgment and be thrown into the fires of Hell. We find this fact supported by Revelation 20:14-15, *"And death and the grave were thrown into the lake of fire. This is the second death—the lake of fire. And anyone whose name was not found recorded in the Book of Life was thrown into the lake of fire."*

But the reality of Hell doesn't have to be so for John 3:16 has just assured us that if we believe in Jesus as the only Son of God, we shall not die but shall have eternal life in heaven with Him. For we also know according to John 14:2-4, that Jesus will go to heaven and prepare a place for us so that where He is, there we shall also be. All of that has been step one of our two-step process. We have come to a mental understanding that being saved means accepting Jesus Christ by confessing with our mouths and believing in our hearts so that we can go to heaven after this life on Earth is complete and spend eternity with God, our Father.

Now we must come to a rational understanding of what we must *do* to be saved.

This is where many Christians fall short in completing the two-step process of accepting the salvation that God has so graciously given to us. We are quick to say, "We love the Lord." But, if God, however, was looking at our actions alone, what would He believe? Are we showing God, by our actions, that we really understand what it means to believe in our hearts that He is the only Son of God?

Step two of our process is the action of doing something to show our understanding. We will now use the Bible to prove that God also uses a two-step process. We will start with Ephesians 2:8-10 that says: "*God saved you by his special favor when you believed. And you can't take credit for this; it is a gift from God. Salvation is not a reward for the good things we have done, so none of us can boast about it. For we are God's masterpiece. He has created us anew in Christ Jesus, so that we can do the good things he planned for us long ago.*" From this passage we can see:

  ➢   Salvation is a gift from God.
  ➢   God saved us because we believed.
  ➢   We cannot gain salvation through our works.
  ➢   Through our salvation, we are created *anew in Christ Jesus.*
  ➢   We are created *anew* so *we can do the good things he planned for us long ago.*

The first three points, we have taken at face value, and they support step one of our two-step process. However, if we take a closer look at the final two points, we see that we must do something. That is, something must change on the inside of us to complete the salvation gift. The scripture says we must become new in Christ Jesus. That means all of our old actions, behaviors, and ways of thinking must change. For some, the change maybe overnight but, for the rest of us, this change happens over time. It did for me. Even still, change must take place. If there is no change, we must ask whether we are really new in Christ Jesus through salvation. Secondarily, if we are new in Christ Jesus, we have become new so that we may be able to do the things God has planned for our lives.

Even in our world's legal system, a gift is never a completed transaction until both parties to the transaction have done something. That is, the giver of the gift must communicate their willingness to give the gift, and the intended receiver of the gift must acknowledge their willingness to accept the gift through whichever mode of response is required by the giver. The failure of either party to complete this transaction makes the gift null and void.

God has communicated through the Bible his willingness to give us eternal life as a gift. He has asked us to communicate with Him our desire to accept His gift by talking back to Him through our belief in His Son, Jesus Christ. With step one (comprehending the meaning of words) and step two (understanding through our actions) in the forefront of our minds, I have an important question to ask. Have you completed the salvation transaction?

❖❖   Pray with me   ❖❖

God, our prayer right now is that everyone completes the two-step process of accepting Your precious gift of salvation. Let us not just provide You lip service, but let us do what Your Word tells us to do. Let our actions and our behavior confirm that we are changing and are renewing our minds and hearts to hear from You. We know that You are not seeking perfection in us, rather, You are looking for our willing hearts to obey and trust You the more. We want You to look down and see us, Your sons and daughters, in whom You are well pleased. We love You Lord and we thank You once again for Your precious gift of salvation that we wholeheartedly accept.
In the name of Jesus, we pray, AMEN.

❖

CHAPTER TWO

What Does It Mean To Believe?

I remember a time when my daughter, Kimberly, was younger and had a birthday party. Children came and brought her gifts. Kimberly readily accepted the gifts as she opened them, except one. She just did not like this particular gift. She wanted to give the gift back and not accept it. After talking privately with her, we eventually got her to understand, "You thank everyone for whatever they give you because they did not have to bring you a gift at all." The point here is that although someone offers you a gift, you do not have to accept the gift. In the same way, simply being offered the gift of salvation does not save you. You must accept the gift. It is through your actions that God knows that you have accepted His gift.

John 1:12 declares, *"But to all who believed him and accepted him, he gave the right to become children of God."*

Why are our actions so important? Actions are important because even Jesus in Matthew 7:15-20 pronounces, *"Beware of false prophets who come disguised as harmless sheep but are really wolves that will tear you apart. You can detect them by the way they act, just as you can identify a tree by its fruit. You don't pick grapes from*

15

thorn bushes, or figs from thistles. A healthy tree produces good fruit, and an unhealthy tree produces bad fruit. A good tree can't produce bad fruit, and a bad tree can't produce good fruit. So every tree that does not produce good fruit is chopped down and thrown into the fire. Yes, the way to identify a tree or a person is by the kind of fruit that is produced."

God has communicated His willingness to give us the gift of salvation by sacrificing His only Son, Jesus Christ on a cross. What are our actions telling Him? Do our actions say to him that we believe Jesus Christ arose from the dead on the third day? Are we bearing good fruit? We can once again go to many scriptures that explain what it means to believe in Jesus Christ. We will raise a few for points of discussion and support here.

Let us first look at John 21:15-17. In this passage, Jesus is asking Simon Peter if he loves him. Jesus asks Peter three separate times if Peter loves him. If you read the passage, you will find that it was not enough for Peter to just respond with, *"You know I love you."* For Jesus says to Peter, *"If you love me, feed my lambs."* Then again, Jesus says to Peter, *"If you love me, feed my sheep."* What is Jesus saying to Peter? Although there may be many interpretations from theologians on the point Jesus was making, all scholars will agree that Jesus required Peter to *do* something to show that he loved Jesus. The same applies to you and me as Christians. We must continually ask ourselves, what are we doing for Jesus to show Him that we believe in Him as required in Romans 10:9?

Some Christians may argue that it is enough to say, "We believe in Christ," and that no works are necessary. Remember, as we have previously shared, understanding is paramount before one can begin to respond with the appropriate action. We need to stop here to refocus and reiterate the points we are making.

➢ We know that works cannot earn us salvation. We are not saying that it does; and,

➢ We know that salvation is a gift from God.

In this chapter, we are discussing how to show God that we truly believe in our hearts, as is required, that He is the Son of God. We have proof in James 2:19-20 that shows it is simply not enough to say we believe. We find these words: *"Do you still think it's enough just to believe that there is one God? Well, even the demons believe this, and they tremble in terror! Fool! When will you ever learn that faith that does not result in good deeds is useless?"*

This scripture shows us that even the demons believe that there is one true God. The demons have spoken with their mouths that they believe there is only one true God. So can we easily say that talking and saying that we believe is enough? We need to once again, reiterate, {this is essential} that we are *not* saying that good deeds will gain salvation. Please keep that distinction clear. Nothing earns salvation except God's grace and mercy. What we are trying to show is that we must do something to show God that we have accepted His gift of salvation. This passage from James 2:19 also implies this as it proves that the demons speak and believe that Jesus is the Son of God. However, we know that the demons will not gain salvation. Is this then a contradiction in the Bible? For the Word of God says if we believe, we will be saved. Of course not! That is why it is so important that we complete the process of accepting the gift. Demons do not complete the process because their actions show that although they can receive salvation, they have chosen not to accept the gift. What do your actions show?

The passage in James also lifts up the word, "Faith." Faith is synonymous with believing. Webster's Dictionary defines belief as having faith in, trust or confidence. Therefore, wherever we see the word faith, trust, or belief in the Bible, they can be interchangeable. This is important to know because James 2:17 says that someone saying they have faith is no good if no good deeds (or actions) come from their faith.

"Once when he {Jesus} was in the synagogue, a man possessed by a demon began shouting at Jesus, 'Go away!

Why are you bothering us, Jesus of Nazareth? Have you come to destroy us? I know who you are—the Holy One sent from God.'" Even the demons in Luke 4:33-34 know and believe that Jesus is the Holy One, the Son of God.

So what are these scriptures saying to you? If knowing and believing is enough, why are the demons not saved? Yes, God has offered His gift of salvation to demons. However, they have chosen not to accept His gift. This point cannot be stressed enough times. Please do not allow your actions to say to God that you do not want to accept His gift of salvation as the demons have done. Please do not let a tradition of teaching that says, "God knows your heart," to cloud your understanding of the process. Again, how many husbands have been heard saying, "You know I love you," when speaking to their wives. Then the wife responds, "How am I suppose to know? Your actions don't say to me that you love me!" Remember, Jesus told Peter to show Him, by doing something, not just saying it.

In James 2:14-18 we see faith without actions is discussed further. *"Dear brothers and sisters, what's the use of saying you have faith if you don't prove it by your actions? That kind of faith can't save anyone. Suppose you see a brother or sister who needs food or clothing, and you say, 'Well good-bye and God bless you; stay warm and eat well'— but then you don't give that person any food or clothing.*

What good does that do? So you see, it isn't enough just to have faith. Faith that doesn't show itself by good deeds is no faith at all—it is dead and useless. Now someone may argue, 'Some people have faith; others have good deeds.' I say, 'I can't see your faith if you don't have good deeds, but I will show you my faith through my good deeds."

I believe we as Christians have for far too long been giving only lip service to our Lord and Savior, Jesus Christ. We say, "We love the Lord." We recite Romans 10:9 almost in a robotic tone without actually thinking about the truth of what it means to believe in Jesus Christ. We walk up the aisle on Sunday mornings to join a church, and we do exactly that, join a church. Read this next line carefully. *Please do not confuse all these actions with your salvation.* Prayerfully I have shown through scripture that merely speaking words are not enough. Let us remember First John 3:18-20, *"Dear children, let us stop just saying we love each other; let us really show it by our actions. It is by our actions that we know we are living in the truth, so we will be confident when we stand before the Lord, even if our hearts condemn us. For God is greater than our hearts, and he knows everything."*

❖❖ Let's Pray ❖❖

Lord, please forgive me if I have sent the wrong message to You and to those who may have observed my spiritual walk. I ask and I thank You for giving me fresh revelation and the courage that's needed so I may be more sensitive to my actions and behavior, especially those that are not pleasing to You. I love You Lord and I thank You for loving me. I pray this prayer in the name that is above all names, in Jesus name, I pray, AMEN.

CHAPTER THREE

❖❖❖

*The Unbeliever, Immature & Mature Christian
Who Are They?*

Unbeliever, Immature Christian and Mature Christian are terms that will be repeated throughout this book. To fully appreciate the contexts of how each word is utilized, it is vital to our understanding that they are defined. There will be distinct differences in each person depending on where they are in their faith walk. Hence a definition will be used to associate each behavior to understand how I have classified them.

No one would disagree that in life in general, most do not copy the behaviors of children or infants. For we all recognize their behavior as appropriate for their age only. But as they get older, one would expect their behavior to resemble an adult; not an adult still behaving like a child. Each of us should be striving to be the Mature Christian as Philippians 3:15-18 says, *"I hope all of you who are Mature Christians will agree on these things. If you disagree on some point, I believe God will make it plain to you. But we must be sure to obey the truth we have learned already. Dear brothers and sisters, pattern your lives after mine, and learn from those who follow our example. For I have told you often before, and I say it again with tears in my eyes, that there are many whose conduct shows they are really enemies of the cross of Christ."*

As you read the definitions below, see if you can determine which category best fits your daily walk with Christ.

Unbeliever:

An Unbeliever is an individual who has not accepted Jesus Christ as their Lord and Savior in agreement with Romans 10:9. The behavior of the Unbeliever: They watch those who profess to be a Christian.

Immature Christian:

An Immature Christian is an individual who has acknowledged Jesus in agreement with Romans 10:9. The behavior of the Immature Christian: The Immature Christian is like a very young child that must be taught and is learning right from wrong. He or she is expected to make mistakes. Likened to a child, the Immature Christian will probably touch the hot stove or run into the street without looking both ways. But God will deal with them as parents deal with their young children. Immature Christians, like young children to their parents, look to the Mature Christians in the church to show them the correct way to live and to act.

Mature Christian:

A Mature Christian is someone who has accepted Christ as their Lord and Savior and is allowing the Holy Spirit to use them as living examples.

The behavior of the Mature Christian: Mature Christians strive to get closer to God and to learn more about our Lord and Savior. Colossians 3:10 says, *"In its place you have clothed yourselves with a brand-new nature that is continually being renewed as you learn more and more about Christ, who created this new nature within you."*

Mature Christians hunger and thirst for wisdom and knowledge. They read their Word, talk to God daily, and seek His will for their lives. They also recognize their lives as imperfect; yet, they willingly adjust their lifestyles with every new revelation from God. Each time God reveals a new way of living or a new way of thinking, a Mature Christian is ready to change his or her lifestyle so that ultimately it is God who is pleased and not man.

Maturity as a Christian has nothing to do with the number of years you have been alive, saved, or in a church. Maturity has everything to do with the length of time you have turned your entire life over to God's will and not your will. It is the Mature Christian that God holds accountable to instruct Immature Christians on Godly behavior. What are you, those who call yourselves the Mature Christian, teaching the Immature Christians who are watching you? Believe me; they are watching you. Are you pointing them toward good, godly behavior or the ways and customs of this world?

❖ ❖   Prayer(s)   ❖ ❖

For the Unbeliever

God, I am a sinner, and I desire to be saved. I confess with my mouth that Jesus is Lord and believe in my heart that God raised Jesus from the dead. I accept You, Jesus, as my Lord and Savior and receive Your gift of salvation.
In the Name of Jesus, I pray, AMEN.

Date: _____ _____, 20 _____
             (Month)   (Day)   (Year)

For the Immature Christian

Lord, protect me from my ignorance. Keep back the tricks of the adversary who desires to tempt me away from the truth of Christ during my infancy stages. I want to grow stronger in You, and I need Your help, guidance, and support. Please show me Mature Christians to follow and emulate.
In the Name of Jesus, I pray, AMEN.

For the Mature Christian

Lord, God, help me to not be a distraction or deterrent to an Unbeliever or Immature Christian. I desire to be an example and role model for them to follow. Protect me and keep me focused knowing that what I say and do, can and will impact others You have sent for me to assist. I live for You and Your blessings, not man. I look forward to that day when I hear You say, well done my good and faithful servant.
In the Name of Jesus, I pray, AMEN.

25

CHAPTER FOUR

Living The Life Of A Saved Christian

I f you are anything like me, I want to know what the life of a saved Christian looks like. We have discussed thus far from scripture what it means to receive God's gift of salvation and what actions, (how we are living our lives,) show God that we have accepted His gift. Now let's take some time and look at the life of a saved Christian.

"And all who believe this will keep themselves pure, just as Christ is pure. Those who sin are opposed to the law of God, for all sin opposes the law of God. And you know that Jesus came to take away our sins, for there is no sin in him. So if we continue to live in him, we won't sin either. But those who keep on sinning have never known him or understood who he is." (1 John 3:3-6)

We just read that those of us who have an eager expectation to be like Christ will keep ourselves pure and will not continually sin. So, what does it mean to keep ourselves "pure?" Looking once again at Merriam-Webster's Dictionary, we find the word pure defined as "Unmixed with other matter, not harsh or rough, free from taint, or containing nothing that does not properly belong." If we then apply these definitions to our lifestyles, then we are saying we are making an honest effort not to do the things that do not properly fit or conform to the lifestyle of a saved Christian. We are free from being tainted by the desires of our flesh or other worldly endeavors. Verse six identifies a Christian who continually sins as someone who does not know God and or understood who He is. One could easily conclude just from this passage then, that someone who continually sins would not be called a Christian. However, I know making that statement here would cause every theologian to discount everything previously written in this book because we know that the scripture also tells us that *all have sinned and come short of the glory of God* (Romans 3:23). So we must discuss the statement in greater detail.

First, we can use the example found so often in the Bible, and that is the analogy of a parent and child. God is our parent, our Father and we are His children. As a parent, we often give our children a list of chores or responsibilities that they are required to do on a daily basis around the house. The list could contain things like cleaning a bathroom and taking out the trash. If we, as the parent, return from work to find that the garbage has not been taken out on day one, most parents would remind the child that they were supposed to take the trash out.

27

However, if on day two, we return home to see that once again the trash was not taken out, we might be just a little upset and once again ask our child if they understood that they are required to take the trash out every day. In most cases, the child will answer, "Yes," they understand. We then walk away feeling confident, believing that taking out the trash will no longer be a problem. But needless to say, day three, four, five, and six come along, and each of those days the trash is still in the house. We finally reach the conclusion that our child has made a decision that they are not going to do what we have asked them to do. They know better; but have chosen, intentionally, to be disobedient. It's the same way we are with God. Look at First John 3:3-6 again.

Yes, all have sinned, but are you doing the same sin over and over again or a different one? How you answer this question is paramount! If you are continually sinning with the same sin that God has made clear to you not to do and you have received the revelation and conviction that it is a sin...then perhaps you have made an intentional decision to be disobedient to the Word of God. You are not, by your consistent actions, trying to please God. Admit the truth. You are living for yourself and doing what you desire to do regardless of whether it is acceptable to God. (Ouch, that hurt didn't it?)

Let's go a step further with our example with the child failing to take out the trash. For illustrative purposes, the child failed to take the trash out on day one but on day two the trash was taken out; but now the bed is not made. While the parent will still likely be upset with the bed not made, clearly from this example, the parent will be delighted that at least the trash is out. A gentle reminder will be given in most cases by the parent to remind the child that the bed must also be made up. On day three that same parent can come home, and the trash is out, the bed is neat, but now clothes are all over the floor. Once again, in most cases, the parent may be getting a little annoyed with the child; but the parent is beginning to see progress in the child trying to do all the things that have been emphasized as important to the parent. Since God is our Father, we can safely assume, He feels the same way when He looks at us. Yes, we were sinners (before Christ) and (after Christ) we sin perhaps every day. However, what we want Him to see, as He looks at us, is a child who may have sinned yesterday; but the sin of today is different. That is, we understand what is pleasing to Him and we make a decision not to do the things He has revealed to us as not pleasing to Him. That does not mean we are perfect; but it does mean that we are trying to get our relationship with God right and we do so by being obedient to His rules, His regulations, and His commands for which we have received the revelation and conviction to correct.

Galatians 5:22-23 shows us that, *"When the Holy Spirit controls our lives, he will produce this kind of fruit in us: love, joy, peace, patience, kindness, goodness, faithfulness, gentleness, and self-control."* If we allow the fruit of the Spirit to control our lives; our thinking and actions, we would not be as tempted to sin.

As you look at the fruit of the spirit, don't get discouraged if you have not developed all nine of these fruit to the point that they are all ripe and ready to be eaten. None of us are there. That's perfection, and no one is ever perfect. God knows that for some of us our fruit is still green and inedible. For others, no fruit is even visible; however, if we examine a little closer we might see a bud or two beginning to blossom. The point is, we should all be striving to grow the fruit of the Holy Spirit, which governs our behavior that is pleasing to God. Who can hate their neighbor when they have the fruit of love? Who can start an argument, when they have the fruit of peace? Who can be mean and stubborn, when they have the fruit of goodness and kindness? Who can commit adultery when they have the fruit of faithfulness? Who cannot have compassion for their brother, when they have the fruit of gentleness? Who cannot have the discipline and fortitude to resist temptation when they have the fruit of self-control?

Conversely, there is similar fruit for those who have decided not to live for Christ. Galatians 5:19-21 tells us what their lives resemble: *"When you follow the desires of your sinful nature, your lives will produce these evil results: sexual immorality, impure thoughts, eagerness for lustful pleasure, idolatry, participation in demonic activities, hostility, quarreling, jealousy, outbursts of anger, selfish ambition, divisions, the feeling that everyone is wrong except those in your own little group, envy, drunkenness, wild parties, and other kinds of sin."*

All sin generates from the fruit or the results of following our sinful nature and shows us where unacceptable fruit or behavior is rooted. The fruit of committing adultery (one of the Ten commandments) is rooted in sexual immorality. Porn is rooted in the fruit of impure thoughts. Orgies and getting drunk is rooted in the fruit of eagerness for lustful pleasures. Practicing witchcraft and manipulation is rooted in the fruit of participation in demonic activities. Mean and hateful spirits are rooted in the fruit of hostility. Always fighting and arguing is rooted in the fruit of quarreling. Having to have your way is rooted in the fruit of selfish ambition. The list of unacceptable behavior and actions can be traced back to the fruit grown from not allowing the Holy Spirit to control our lives.

What fruit are you allowing to grow in your life? What does your life resemble when compared to these two very different fruit of the spirit? If you find yourself repeatedly displaying more of the fruit of a sinful nature, you have to ask yourself if you have wholly accepted Jesus Christ into your heart and your life, allowing the Holy Spirit to begin a good work in you through His fruit of the spirit. You have to ask the Holy Spirit to control your life daily. The completed two-step process (by showing in your actions plus your behavior) will be the evidence that good fruit is growing in you and that the good fruit is controlling your Christian life.

"Finally, dear brothers and sisters, we urge you in the name of the Lord Jesus to live in a way that pleases God, as we have taught you." (1 Thessalonians 4:1)

I can't emphasize enough that no one is without sin. It is true that all have sinned *but* what is *not* true is that we have been given a license to continue sinning. No, this is the devil's cunning way of keeping us from striving to follow the principles of the Bible and making us think if we can't follow them all then there is no use in continuing to try because we can never reach perfection. God is not looking for perfection. No one can ever be perfect. God

seeks for the person who is earnest to follow His ⌐
principles and refuses to continue doing that thing that
does not please God. Don't allow Immature Christians or
Unbelievers to use this logic to excuse their behavior or
ours.

*"So put to death the sinful, earthly things lurking within
you. Have nothing to do with sexual sin, impurity, lust, and
shameful desires. Don't be greedy for the good things of this
life, for that is idolatry. God's terrible anger will come upon
those who do such things. You used to do them when your life
was still part of this world. But now is the time to get rid of
anger, rage, malicious behavior, slander, and dirty language.
Don't lie to each other, for you have stripped off your old evil
nature and all its wicked deeds. In its place, you have clothed
yourselves with a brand-new nature that is continually
renewing as you learn more and more about Christ, who
created this new nature within you."* Colossians 3:5-10
helps us to understand that our Christian living and
lifestyle (to live it as God desires and not as our flesh
desires) is a daily challenge. We must challenge our flesh
regularly to do the right thing, think the right way, and let
our life be an example of what God would want others to
see in us and through our actions.

Romans 12:1-2 is another good scripture to support
what a Christian lifestyle should model. *"And so, dear
brothers and sisters, I plead with you to give your bodies to*

33

God. Let them be a living and holy sacrifice—the kind he will accept. When you think of what he has done for you, is this too much to ask? Don't copy the behavior and customs of this world, but let God transform you into a new person by changing the way you think. Then you will know what God wants you to do and you will know how good and pleasing and perfect his will really is."

After reading this passage of scripture, we can identify some beginning points on Christian living:

➢ A Christian's life should exemplify the life and teachings of Jesus Christ so that others might desire to be saved.

➢ A Christian should live their life so that others (Unbelievers and Immature Christians) may see a difference in one who claims to be a Mature Christian and one who is an Unbeliever.

➢ A Christian must not imitate the world's model of behavior or seek its approval.

➢ A Christian often talks to God (reading the Bible) allowing Him to renew their thinking about what is right and wrong in their Christian walk and lifestyle.

➢ A Christian's lifestyle is acceptable to God.

I'm reminded of what an unknown author once said, "You can do whatever you want, as long as what you do pleases God."

Romans 13:13 states, *"We should be decent and true in everything we do so that everyone can approve of our behavior."*

Decent and true does not mean to be a hypocrite. You must lead one life instead of double lives. What kind of a witness can you be for Christ, when one set of your friends see you saying and doing one thing with them, and then they watch you refusing to do those same things when your Christian brothers and sisters come around? No wonder Unbelievers and Immature Christians are confused when they see Mature Christians behaving this way.

Even Paul, in Galatians 2:11-13, had to admonish Peter for being a hypocrite. *"But when Peter came to Antioch, I had to oppose him publicly, speaking strongly against what he was doing, for it was very wrong. When he first arrived, he ate with the Gentile Christians, who don't bother with circumcision. But afterward, when some Jewish friends of James came, Peter wouldn't eat with the Gentiles anymore because he was afraid of what these legalists would say. Then the other Jewish Christians followed Peter's hypocrisy, and even Barnabas was influenced to join them in their hypocrisy."*

Paul was apparently upset with Peter because he was attempting to lead a double life. How many of you are living a life like Peter? Are there things that you do with your friends that you do not do in front of your pastor? Are you not doing it because you think it is wrong? Or are there other reasons for you changing your behavior? How you answer these two questions is tantamount to your being a Mature Christian living a lifestyle acceptable to Christ.

❖ ❖ Prayer ❖ ❖

Dear God, hear our prayer. Help us to cultivate a garden of holy, spiritual fruit. We want the kind of fruit that will enable us to display godly behavior and actions that make You smile. Give us the strength and help us to weed out any dead fruit of a sinful nature that we know can grow with no assistance, no watering, and with no nourishment. We recognize that we must be intentional in allowing spiritual fruit to grow within us. Help us, oh Lord, to nourish this garden for we want a full harvest of peace, love, joy, patience, goodness, faithfulness, gentleness, kindness, and self-control to operate in our lives. With these fruit of the Spirit, we will be better equipped to escape the temptation of sin that leads to unacceptable behavior and actions that are contrary to a saved Christian trying to show that we have accepted Your gift of salvation. In the name of Jesus, we pray, Amen.

❖

CHAPTER FIVE

The Do's & Don'ts Of Christian Behavior

A s a child of God, we have inherited certain rights and privileges that come with being in the family of Christ. One of those privileges is salvation. However, as we discussed in the previous chapter, we also know being a part of a family also requires rules and regulations. In most healthy families, children have responsibilities. These responsibilities may include cleaning their rooms, sweeping, or any other number of duties. Also included in the rules and regulations are a list of do's and don'ts. These do's and don'ts are for the good of the children and are designed to protect and guide them from hurt, harm, and danger. They are also beneficial so the children will mature into responsible adults able to raise healthy children of their own in the future. And most importantly, rules and regulations are needed, so the kids know the things that are pleasing (or displeasing) to their parents.

So, how do we as children of God learn the do's and don'ts of Mature Christian behavior so that we can develop from Immature Christian to Mature Christian just as in the physical we grow from infant to toddler, to teenager, to adulthood? As Christians, we need to know, at all stages of our growth, what behavior is pleasing and displeasing to Christ. In the natural, we look to our parents to teach us the standards, character, and behavior they desire to see in us as their children. Much like our natural parents, God, our Father, has left us His Holy Word to instruct us in all aspects of our lives. For we find these words in Second Timothy 3:16, *"All scripture is inspired by God and is useful to teach us what is true and to make us realize what is wrong in our lives. It straightens us out and teaches us to do what is right."* And so it is that we should be able to use the sixty-six books of scripture to inform us on our behavior through the stages of our growth in the Lord, Jesus Christ.

It is important to stop here and reiterate that we are not talking about do's and don'ts that relate to our salvation. Do's and don'ts cannot get us saved. We are talking about our actions *after* having accepted God's gift of salvation. Those who do not need this repeated, please forgive the author; however, there are many Christians who keep interchanging these two points and thus cause discord when talking about Christian behavior and works.

Some Christians will say, "Sinning should include do's and don'ts." But what is sin? Remember, we have been clear that the purpose of this book is to be sure we understand the words that we use so that we are not just giving lip service to answers, but that we accept with certainty what we are saying. So, what is sin? The word, sin is defined in the Tyndale Publishing House's New Living Translation of the Bible as, "To miss the mark, or fall short of God's level of perfection; to break God's commands." This definition is supported by First John 3:7-9. *"Dear children, don't let anyone deceive you about this: When people do what is right, it is because they are righteous, even as Christ is righteous. But when people keep on sinning, it shows they belong to the Devil, who has been sinning since the beginning. Those who have been born into God's family do not sin because God's life is in them. So they can't keep on sinning because they have been born of God. So now we can tell who are children of God and who are children of the Devil. Anyone who does not obey God's commands and does not love other Christians does not belong to God."*

From this scripture we see the following:

➢ We are born into God's family through acceptance of Romans 10:9.
➢ If we are in God's family, we cannot keep on sinning.
➢ Children in God's family obey God's commands.
➢ Children in God's family love other Christians.

So, if sin is missing the mark or not following the commands of God, we as Christians must know what the commands of God are to follow and obey them. Some Christians would immediately go to Exodus and other books of the Bible that talk about the Law as the commands of God. We know that the books of Exodus, Deuteronomy, Numbers, and Leviticus outline a lot of the do's and don'ts of God or in simple terms, the commands, rules, and regulations God desire for us to follow. However, since we are going to talk about commands, rules, and regulations, found in the Old Testament, we must pause here and clarify yet another area of great debate about whether or not the Old Testament is relevant and applicable to us as Christians today.

We find these words in Galatians 3:19, *"Well then, why was the law given? It was given to show people how guilty they are."*

That is, the Law was given so that people would know what upsets God. The Law was given to protect the people and bring them to righteousness until Jesus Christ was born and could save them through His death, burial, and resurrection. Even Jesus in Matthew 5:17-19 declares, *"Don't misunderstand why I have come. I did not come to abolish the law of Moses or the writings of the prophets. No, I came to fulfill them. I assure you, until heaven and Earth* disappear, even the smallest detail of God's law will remain until its purpose is achieved. So if you break the smallest commandment and teach others to do the same, you will be the least in the Kingdom of Heaven. But anyone who obeys God's laws and teaches them will be great in the Kingdom of Heaven."

We know, however, that even before the Law people knew right from wrong. How is it that people knew right from wrong even before the Law? We need only look to the entire book of Genesis where men and women of God followed God's commands, laws, and regulations. Romans 2:13-16 answers the question for us by saying: *"For it is not merely knowing the law that brings God's approval. Those who obey the law will be declared right in God's sight. Even when Gentiles, who do not have God's written law, instinctively follow what the law says, they show that in their hearts they know right from wrong. They demonstrate that God's law is written within them, for their own consciences either accuse them or tell them they are doing what is right. The day will surely come when God, by Jesus Christ, will judge everyone's secret life."*

Also, Romans 7:7 answers why God's Law shows us God's list of do's and don'ts. For the passage of Romans reads: *"Well then, am I suggesting that the law of God is evil? Of course not! The law is not sinful, but it was the law*

41

that showed me my sin. I would never have known that coveting is wrong if the law had not said, "Do not covet."

So, as Christians we should be striving to live our lives following the commands, rules, and regulations of God; not because it will bring us salvation, but because it is pleasing to Him. It is only through God providing us His Law that we know what is right and wrong in the sight of God.

Reviewing the Law and how we as Christians should apply it to our lives is perhaps as difficult as talking about tithes, offerings, and first fruit. Somewhere, somehow, we have been miseducated and have built a massive wall separating our ability to comprehend any scripture that is not the Good News or God's Grace and Mercy. My prayer as you have read this book is that your mind, heart, and ears, have been open to the revelation of the words. For we find that even the Apostle Paul recognized the stubbornness of the people to be receptive to the law as recorded in Second Corinthians 3:14-15. *"But the people's minds were hardened, and even to this day whenever the old covenant is being read, a veil covers their minds so they cannot understand the truth. And this veil can be removed only by believing in Christ. Yes, even today when they read Moses' writings, their hearts are covered with that veil, and they do not understand."*

We want you to understand, comprehend, and begin to live the life God so desires for you to live. You cannot start to enjoy the benefits and blessings as a child of God until you open your heart and your mind to His Word as recorded in all the books of the Bible. Let us begin to show God that we do in fact love him. In the book of John chapter fourteen verse twenty-one, we find: *"Those who obey my commandments are the ones who love me. And because they love me, my Father will love them, and I will love them. And I will reveal myself to each one of them."*

❖ ❖ Prayer ❖ ❖

God, I thank You for Your Word. I know You wrote every word written from Genesis in the Old Testament to Revelation in the New Testament for my benefit and for my success. Forgive me, oh Lord, for only reading the parts that I want to adhere to. I desire to live a blessed life and I know that can only be achieved by following all of Your commands, rules and regulations. In the name of Jesus, I pray, AMEN.

❖

CHAPTER SIX

How Your Behavior Impacts Your Rewards In Heaven

S alvation (believing) and our actions go hand in hand. They are not inseparable. We now understand that God's grace and mercy have provided a gift of eternal life to each of us if we would only accept His gift. Many Christians have accepted His gracious offer to spend eternity worshipping Him in spirit and truth. Our prayer, however, is that all Christians now understand that what we do after accepting His gift of salvation will not only show God we have accepted his gift of salvation. But, will be a beacon of light for the Unbeliever and the Immature Christians who are watching us to learn what to do, how to act, and how to live godly lives. Also, how we live our lives (what we do and say) after accepting Jesus Christ will have an impact on our rewards once we reach Heaven.

For the last time, the point will be made that what you do has no bearing on your ability to go to heaven. However, what you *do* will show God that you are His child and will have a bearing on the reward(s) you will receive while still on Earth and when you reach heaven.

So, as Christians destined for heaven, we must ask ourselves the question, "Is it enough to only go to heaven?" That question is not to belittle going to heaven at all. One needs only to read Revelation 20:12-13 to know that once we who are saved reach heaven, we will each be given our rewards. Let's read the scripture for ourselves. *"I saw the dead, both great and small, standing before God's throne. And the books were opened, including the Book of Life. And the dead were judged according to the things written in the books, according to what they had done. The sea gave up the dead in it, and death and the grave gave up the dead in them. They were all judged according to their deeds."*

This passage says, and the books were opened. How many books are there going to be in heaven? One can assume that there must be at least two books since the scripture says, *"And the books were opened, including the Book of Life."* The Book of Life that is mentioned above records the names of all who will be saved and delivered from the lake of fire and eternal damnation. But have we ever stopped to think that there might be other books that record our deeds and actions?

Given the fact that there will be at least two books, you should ponder at least two questions:

> Is your name recorded in The Book of Life? (You know from Romans 10:9 how to get your name from being erased from the Book of Life.)

> Is your name recorded in The Book of Deeds?

While the Holy writ does not name the second book as the Book of Deeds, Revelation 20:12 makes clear that there will be a book that has recorded all the deeds/actions of Christians. It is from this book that rewards will be determined. Revelation 20:13 states, *"They were all judged according to their deeds."*

So, when your judgment time comes, will you be upset with other Christian brothers and sisters who have done more than you and got a greater reward in heaven? For this is what is currently happening in the world today. Christian brothers and sisters are upset and jealous over one another's blessings here on Earth, but it does not have to be so. Read Deuteronomy 8:6-18. *"So obey the commands of the LORD your God by walking in his ways and fearing him. For the LORD your God is bringing you into a good land of flowing streams and pools of water, with springs that gush forth in the valleys and hills. It is a land of wheat and barley, of grapevines, fig trees, pomegranates, olives, and honey. It is a land where food is plentiful, and nothing is lacking. It is a land where iron is as common as stone, and copper is abundant in the hills. When you have eaten your* fill, praise the LORD your God for the good land he has given you. But that is the time to be careful! Beware that in your plenty you do not forget the LORD your God and disobey his commands, regulations, and laws. For when you have become full and prosperous and have built fine homes to live in, and when your flocks and herds have become very large, and your silver and gold have multiplied along with everything else, that is the time to be careful. Do not become proud at that time and forget the LORD your God, who rescued you from slavery in the land of Egypt. Do not forget that he led you through the great and terrifying wilderness with poisonous snakes and scorpions, where it was so hot and dry. He gave you water from the rock! He fed you with manna in the wilderness, a food unknown to your ancestors. He did this to humble you and test you for your own good. He did it so you would never think that it was your own strength and energy that made you wealthy. Always remember that it is the LORD your God who gives you power to become rich, and he does it to fulfill the covenant he made with your ancestors."*

Deuteronomy chapter 8 alone shows that God wants us to prosper while here on Earth. He wants us to be blessed spiritually and materially; however, we must remember Him by giving Him thanks for all He has allowed to come into our lives. Mature Christian brothers and sisters by faith, are reading the entire Bible now and realizing they can enjoy heaven here on Earth, be prosperous in all we do and with all that we possess by following principles outlined in the Bible.

While this book is not focused on prosperity teaching, this is a good place to expound on that subject just a little since the objective of this chapter is our reward once heaven is achieved. Prosperity preaching and teaching has received widespread negative connotations in and outside the Body of Christ. It's hard to see why the Body of Christ is so opposed to believing in the principles of prosperity preaching and teaching found throughout the Bible. This is probably because of some of the manipulation of the principles and scripture that have taken place. No one denies that the Body of Christ has some bad apples in leadership positions; however, there are bad doctors, lawyers, teachers, etc., but we don't stop using them. Rather, we adjust and find a reputable professional in that particular field. The same holds true for the church. Find an integrable preacher and teacher whom can be trusted and follow their leadership. Contrary to popular debates, the Good Book is clear on the lifestyle God desired for his chosen people to experience. In Genesis 2, we find Adam and Eve living in the Garden of Eden, God's chosen place for them. The Garden of Eden had everything Adam and Eve needed to live a prosperous life. All kinds of fruit trees and animals lived there. Genesis 2:10-12 goes on to describe the Garden of Eden this way: *"A river flowed from the land of Eden, watering the garden and then dividing into four branches. One of these branches is the Pishon, which flows around the entire land of Havilah, where gold is found. The gold of that land is exceptionally pure; aromatic resin and onyx stone are also found there."*

In all the splendor of the Garden of Eden, God only required that Adam and Eve not touch the tree of good and evil (Genesis 2:17). Adam and Eve had access to all the gold, onyx stones, and other precious metals found within the Garden. If God did not want Adam or Eve to adorn themselves with gold (jewelry, etc.) why did God not make this a requirement as well? He did not! Therefore, we can conclude to have gold and other precious stones and metals is not forbidden by God. But we don't have to stop here with Adam and Eve.

If we follow the lineage of Adam and Eve, we find the children of Israel were slaves in the land of Egypt for over four hundred years. God heard their cry for help and sent Moses to rescue his chosen people. After four hundred years of slavery, being set free meant starting from the beginning with nothing. However, that was not God's intent for the children of Israel, nor the Gentiles, who will later be offered the same privileges as the Israelites. Exodus 12:34-36 tells us that God caused the Egyptians to be afraid of the Israelites to the point that the Egyptians gave all of their gold, silver, fine linens, and silks (all that they asked for) to them before they left the land of Egypt. So once again, God blessed his people with abundance. *"So like a victorious army, they (the Israelites) plundered the Egyptians!"* If God did not desire for his people to live with abundance, why did God see the need to bless them with the spoils of Egypt? Needless to say, even after being rescued from four hundred years of slavery, and being blessed with riches beyond imagination, the Israelites were once again disobedient to the commands, rules, and regulations of God. The freed Israelites had to wander in the wilderness for forty years. God decided that everyone over the age of twenty-five could not enter the Promised Land. After forty years, when those over the age of twenty-five had died, God allowed the remaining Israelites to enter into the Promised Land. That Promised Land was described above in Deuteronomy 8. It was God's intent for His people to live in a land that was flowing with everything they could ever desire including gold, silver, and other material things. God said they could build fine homes to live in and their gold and silver would multiply along with everything they owned. That sounds like great prosperity to me! Nothing was lacking. In fact, it looks very much like the

Garden of Eden, which was God's original intent. This intent had not and has not changed, even today. It has been the people, us, that kept changing and vacillating between following God and following the customs of the world. We make the decisions to follow God one week and the world the next week. We keep disobeying God and His commands, rules, and regulations. If the Bible ended with Deuteronomy 8, and we continued to follow the commands, rules, and regulations of God, we would all be living in a land that most of us would call a land of peace and prosperity. Alas, the Bible does not end with Deuteronomy. As the approach of the end of the Old Testament and continuing to follow the Israelites we find that they chose again and again to forget God and begin to disobey Him. The Israelites go back into bondage awaiting their rescue by God once more.

In the New Testament, God sends Jesus as our rescuer and redeemer for all of our sins. In the New Testament, believers are living for the day when heaven is within our reach. The book of Revelation 21:18-21 describes heaven as follows. *"The wall was made of jasper, and the city was pure gold, as clear as glass. The wall of the city was built on foundation stones inlaid with twelve gems: the first was jasper, the second sapphire, the third agate, the fourth emerald, the fifth onyx, the sixth carnelian, the seventh chrysolite, the eighth beryl, the ninth topaz, the tenth chrysoprase, the eleventh jacinth, the twelfth amethyst. The twelve gates were made of pearls---each gate from a single pearl! And the main street was pure gold, as clear as glass."*

Imagine a city of pure gold. It is clear when reading the Holy Books from Genesis to Revelation that God's original intent for those who choose to follow his commands, rules, and regulations was to live in a land where nothing was lacking, a land of prosperity. This is important enough to repeat, God's intent for you and me has never changed. God's chosen people have been outside of the land of plenty because of their lack of obedience to the commands, rules, and regulations of God.

Today's society seems to blame everything on someone else. It is never the person's decisions (or disobedience) that got them where they are. It's hard to face the fact that everyone (EVERYONE) is the product of all the decisions made in life, good and bad. Failure to do school work ends in the inability to go to college or even finish high school. This limits one's ability to get a good job and make a decent income. Now the same person is mad at the world for their living status but according to them, "It's everybody else's fault." The list goes on and on with the disobedience (not following the commands, regulations, and laws of God) of society that has caused individuals not to live heaven right here on Earth.

The problem is not the prosperity teachings (as long as they are biblically based). The problem is with the disobedience of people to read the Bible and their faithfulness to learn and follow its principles. God is not looking for perfection. He is looking for individuals who have the heart to want to please Him.

Are you that one God is looking for?

❖ ❖ Let's Talk to God ❖❖

Dear Heavenly Father, forgive me for failing to acknowledge You and thanking You for all that I have. I have been disobedient and I have failed You despite the fact that You have always been here for me. Help me to take control of my life and not blame others for any shortcomings or disappointments I may be currently experiencing. Help me to accept responsibilities over areas of my life that I can control. Continue to allow the Holy Spirit to develop the fruit of self-control in my life so that I can manage my finances. I need to be a better steward of my money as Your principles teach me to be. I have been wasteful and I have not been a tither. I have failed to set priorities with my spending, and because of that, I have suffered financially. I also need more self-control in my personal relationships and wisdom in my choice of partners. My lack of self-control in this area has caused pain and a loss of my self-esteem. I need the patience to wait on You knowing that You have a perfect plan for my life.

I want to live in perfect peace in a land that You have prepared especially for me. I need You, Holy Spirit, to grow that nutritious fruit of the Spirit within me so that in due season, they can burst forth. I want to reap the rewards that come with appropriate behavior and actions.
In the name of Jesus, I pray, AMEN.

CHAPTER SEVEN

What Can You Eat Or Not Eat?

"Accept Christians who are weak in faith, and don't argue with them about what they think is right or wrong. For instance, one person believes it is all right to eat anything. But another believer who has a sensitive conscience will eat only vegetables. Those who think it is all right to eat anything must not look down on those who won't. And those who won't eat certain foods must not condemn those who do, for God has accepted them. Who are to condemn God's servants? They are responsible to the Lord, so let him tell them whether they are right or wrong. The Lord's power will help them do as they should." (Romans 14: 1-4)

Far too often, Christians spend too much time arguing over theological do's and don'ts rather than talking to God and seeking His approval about what is appropriate and what is not. The passage above is dealing with Immature or weak Christians getting into a discussion with Mature Christians over food. In Romans chapter 14, Paul tells us that Immature Christians and Mature Christians will think differently and there is nothing wrong with that. However, we, as Mature

Christians, are not to get into arguments with other Christians about things we believe they should not be eating because we believe it is wrong for them to eat certain foods. How many arguments have there been between Jews and Gentiles (Immature and Mature Christians) over pork? Who can turn on their summer grill and not put some pork spare ribs, pork chops, or burnt sausage links on it? Where are the crab-lovers? Raise your hands. I love steamed crabs during the summer months. Living in the Hampton Roads area off of the Chesapeake Bay, it's hard not to enjoy a bushel of hot steamed crabs dusted with just the right amount of old bay seasoning, along with a favorite secret dipping sauce. I can taste them right now. Whether Christians can eat pork or steamed crabs has consistently been a debate. So it is no surprise that this is one question I readily searched the Bible to find the answer to. And Hallelujah, the answer was in Romans 14! It is not a sin to eat pork or steamed crabs as is often quoted by some Christians.

One point that should be made here; however, is just because it may be okay to eat pork or other types of foods, not all foods are good for our diets. The clear distinction to be made is whether or not the consumption is a sin or simply not good for our health. The contention I have with some Christians is that they classify everything they object to as a sin rather than explaining that the choice(s) just may not be good (healthy). These Christians suggest these "sinful" choices will send one to hell, but this is not so! One must use reasonable judgment in deciding whether a particular food or drink is healthy for their diet. An unhealthy diet is not the same as sinning.

Mature Christians read the Bible and try to follow it completely. However, too many Christians have only read select portions of the Bible and have not received revelation on various topics. One can read the Book of Exodus, Leviticus, Numbers, and Deuteronomy and find many such forbidden foods. So, what does all of this mean as it relates to forbidden foods and God's desire for what is right and wrong with certain foods?

Romans 14:6 says, *"Those who eat all kinds of food do so to honor the Lord since they give thanks to God before eating. And those who won't eat everything also want to please the Lord and give thanks to God."*

This means that as Christians we need to be sure that every time we eat, we should be saying our grace. Now we know because of this scripture, yet another reason why saying our grace is so essential. Saying our grace also shows God that we are thankful to him for the food that has been provided. But saying our grace, according to Romans 14:6, furthermore shows God that we are trying to please him with all that we eat. We say to God that what we are eating or not eating is our way of honoring him and that is the point to honor God in our eating.

Sounded too easy, didn't it? Of course, it was. There is more. We need to continue reading the 14th chapter of the book of Romans. Let us look at verses 14-16 then 20-23. *"I know and am perfectly sure on the authority of the Lord Jesus that no food, in and of itself, is wrong to eat. But if someone believes it is wrong, then for that person it is wrong. And if another Christian is distressed by what you eat, you are not acting in love if you eat it. Don't let your eating ruin someone for whom Christ died. Then you will not be condemned for doing something you know is all right."* Verses 20-23: *"Don't tear apart the work of God over what you eat. Remember, there is nothing wrong with these things in themselves. But it is wrong to eat anything if it makes another person stumble. Don't eat meat or drink wine or do anything else if it might cause another Christian to stumble. You may have the faith to believe that there is nothing wrong with what you are doing, but keep it between yourself and God. Blessed are those who do not condemn themselves by doing something they know is all right. But if people have doubts about whether they should eat something, they shouldn't eat it. They would be condemned for not acting in faith before God. If you do anything you believe is not right, you are sinning."*

What is Paul saying here? We just read that it is okay to eat anything and that God is honored if we say our grace before we eat. Also, we see that we as Mature Christians are responsible to the Unbelievers and Immature Christians with our behavior as it relates to the food we eat. Remember our purpose in life as Christians apart from salvation is to live a lifestyle that is pleasing to God and a living example of his love and grace in our lives. That means we are not to eat anything that may cause an Unbeliever or Immature Christian to begin to doubt our Christian walk. For example, if we are with an Unbeliever or young Christian who believes or verbalizes it is ungodly to eat, for example, pork, then we are not to eat pork.

Our goal in life is to bring people closer to God, not away from the Lord because they are not yet at a point in their faith walk to accept that eating pork is okay. Remember the previous passage that says it is not our role to argue with them about whether eating pork is right or wrong. We can offer our opinion and even show them the 14th chapter of Romans. But until they come into the revelation that pork is okay, we are being worthy of our call as Mature Christians to refrain from eating the pork *around them.*

This passage also points out that if we have a doubt about whether something is right or wrong or a sense of uncertainty, we should not indulge. For even if something

we eat is suitable for eating, but we believe it is not right
to eat it then we are committing sin.

❖ ❖　Prayer　❖ ❖

*God, You alone know our hearts. Our ultimate desire is to
please You continually. We constantly need Your help for
without You we are powerless. Help us to understand that
food is primarily to sustain our bodies and provide the
nourishment it needs to keep us strong and healthy. Help us
not to get into godless arguments over whether we can eat
certain foods. Help us to simply remember to love our
brothers for we are our brother's keeper. Help us not to be a
stumbling block regarding food to anyone who may be
watching what we eat. And Lord, as we eat, help us not to be
guilty of gluttony, for it is a sin. Help us to put our forks down
and back away from the table when we are tempted to
overindulge. It is our deepest desire to give You all of the
glory and all of the honor You are so richly deserving of.
Thank You, oh God, Creator of everything that is good and
perfect.　In the name of Jesus, we pray, AMEN.*

❖

CHAPTER EIGHT
❖ ❖ ❖ ❖ ❖ ❖ ❖ ❖
Can You Drink Wine Or Other Alcoholic Beverages?

D o you believe it is wrong to drink wine or other alcoholic beverages? If your answer is yes, then according to Romans 14:23, it is a sin for you to drink wine or other alcoholic beverages. Are you drinking around Unbelievers or Immature Christians who believe it is wrong to drink wine or other alcoholic beverages? If you are, then you are not being a strong, Mature Christian because you are potentially turning them away from Christ if you drink in their presence.

Does the Bible, however, literally say that one cannot drink wine or other alcoholic beverages? Consider the following passages on drinking wine or spirits. In First Timothy 5:23, Paul says to Timothy, *"Don't drink only water. You ought to drink a little wine for the sake of your stomach because you are sick so often."* The great prophet, Paul, is supporting this aspect of drinking as it relates to medical benefits of drinking wine. Some credible physicians today also encourage their patients to drink "A glass of (red) wine" each day for medicinal purposes. In Mathew 11:18-19 Jesus declares, *"For John, the Baptist didn't drink wine, and he often fasted, and you say, 'He's demon possessed.' And I, the Son of Man, feast*

61

and drink, and you say, 'He's a glutton and a drunkard, and a friend of the worst sort of sinners!' But wisdom is shown to be right by what results from it."

This passage raises a critical dialogue about the behavior of Jesus and his acknowledgment that he *"Feasts and drinks."* Jesus, the Christian example we strive to follow, acknowledges that he drank and feasted. I remember when I first came across this passage of scripture. I ran and showed it to my husband. Although he has gone through the Bible many times, he could not believe what he was reading; he could not believe the scripture was there. Did the Bible really just say that Jesus *"Drank and feasted and was called a glutton and a drunkard?"* I think many of us reading this passage would come to the conclusion that if some believed this of Jesus then when there was a party, Jesus was there and he was having fun and drinking alcoholic beverages. Now we know Jesus was without sin for Hebrews 4:15 declares, *"This High Priest of ours understands our weaknesses, for he faced all of the same temptations we do, yet he did not sin."* We know and believe that Jesus was never drunk (for he was without sin), but I am sure because he was partaking of alcoholic beverages, laughing, and having fun, that some may have assumed him to be drunk. I know this passage has caused many to pause and reach for their

Bibles to look this scripture up *and* to make sure I recorded it correctly. Rest assured, I did. If the Bible records this, why are there disagreements about whether or not Christians can drink alcoholic beverages? Jesus drank them. In fact, Jesus in this passage implies that they cannot win whether they drink or don't drink. For Jesus says, John the Baptist did not drink and fasted often, yet people called him crazy. Then he says *"I, the Son of Man, drink and feast and you call me crazy as well!"*

My husband happened to be preaching a sermon where there was a reference to drinking wine and alcoholic beverages. He always takes these opportunities to let our partners know he does not drink nor do I because of the promise I made to him. I don't remember exactly the point he was trying to make, but he ended up saying to the partners that they have double standards when it comes to them as Christians and their pastors as Christians. He asked how many of them would feel 'some kind of a way' if they walked into a restaurant and saw us with a glass of wine or alcoholic beverage? Not surprisingly, quite a few hands went up. When he followed that question up with would they feel the same way if they saw another church partner in that same restaurant having the same alcoholic drink, not surprisingly, the answer was, "No." Why the double standard? There is only one Bible. There is not a Bible for Christian pastors and another Bible for Lay Christians. Christians are Christians, and our behavior and actions should be the same. I believe there may be several reasons for the double standard. I firmly believe based on my time spent in the Baptist church that pastors have taught the church primarily that "Not drinking is 'holy' and drinking is a 'sin,' which will send them to Hell." Since this has been the teaching that has been passed down through many pastoral generations, many pastors believe this to be an accurate and a biblically supported statement. Sadly, however, they have not taken the time to research this topic for themselves and have chosen instead to believe what was taught and modeled before them.

Even Paul in First Corinthians 8:8 articulates, *"It's true that we can't win God's approval by what we eat. We don't miss out on anything if we don't eat, and we don't gain anything if we do."* So clearly, our lifestyle is not about what we eat or drink.

The final passage highlighted on drinking wine and alcoholic beverages is found in the story of Noah in Genesis 9:24. That passage says Noah woke up from his drunkard stupor to find that his sons had been laughing at him. We know that God saved Noah and his family because Noah had found favor with God. For in Genesis 6:9 we see that *"Noah was a righteous man, the* only blameless man living on Earth at the time. He consistently followed God's will and enjoyed a close relationship with him." Do we as Christians today consider people who have drunkard stupors as righteous, blameless people before God? I don't think so, but because God did not use this opportunity to express His disdain for drunkard behavior, I can't help but question how God could call Noah righteous. Especially, by today's standards, a drunk, in most circles, would definitely not be called righteous.

Noah drank, yet in Genesis 9:19, God still chose him to become the Father of man as we know it today. Apparently, his drinking did not stop God from using him; nor is there any record of God saying his drinking was ungodly. God will surely let us know if a particular behavior is unacceptable in the Bible. Before you burn this book on this point, here is an example of God using a situation to identify sin. Consider David when he committed adultery with Bathsheba. Although this story of David is not about drinking alcoholic beverages, it does speak to God using every opportunity in the Bible to call out behavior that is not pleasing to Him. King David was a murderer and an adulterer; however, God still used David. After King David had sinned, God had the prophet, Nathan, tell King David that his behavior was a sin that would have consequences. God acknowledged the sin of

David so that those who would read the Bible would know that God did not condone the behavior of murder and adultery.

There are many more passages of scripture that could have been highlighted to illuminate my point; however, the following will show that the Bible does not say drinking a glass of wine or other alcoholic beverages is a sin or behavior unbecoming a Mature Christian.

It is amazing that God gave Moses very detailed laws on how people should live and behave. These laws are recorded specifically and carefully in the books of Exodus, Leviticus, and Numbers. Yet in none of these books are there instructions, laws, or commands that forbid the drinking of wine or alcoholic beverages. Let's be clear. Drinking and drunk are not the same. For the Bible is explicit on not becoming drunk. Drunk is defined when one has engaged in drinking wine or other alcoholic beverages to the point where they are not in control of their behavior. Most of us use the term, inebriated. We find in Ephesians 5:18 *"Don't be drunk with wine, because that will ruin your life. Instead, let the Holy Spirit fill and control you."*

Galatians 3:19 articulates that God gave the laws in the books of Exodus, Leviticus, and Numbers so that people would know right from wrong or how guilty they were in their actions. Yet in all the detail of these books, once again, God does not say that drinking wine or other alcoholic beverages is a sin. In fact, many of the festivals and celebrations required by God included the drinking of wine. Why do you suppose this is so?

Is it hard to believe that the first miracle Jesus performed at the wedding at Cana would be to change water into wine if drinking wine was a sin? We find that not only did Jesus turn water into wine but it was exceptional wine as recorded in John 2:9-10. *"When the master of ceremonies tasted the water that was now wine, not knowing where the wine had come from (though, of course, the servants knew), he called the bridegroom over. Usually, a host serves the best wine first, he said. Then, when everyone is full and doesn't care, he brings out the less expensive wines. But you have kept the best until now!"*

The last supper is a story well told of Jesus' last supper with his disciples before his crucifixion. Jesus served wine at the last supper. In Luke 22:17, we find these words, *"Then he took a cup of wine, and when he had given thanks for it, he said, 'Take this and share it among yourselves."* It is evident, if drinking wine were a sin, Jesus would not have caused his disciples to sin especially at the Last Supper. In First Peter 2:22, it is incontrovertible that Jesus was without sin. Therefore, one can easily conclude that drinking wine cannot be a sin.

A few Bible scriptures found by this author (the author in no way assumes that there might not be other scriptures) that specifically addresses no drinking is found in Numbers 6:3 and Luke 1:15.

In Numbers 6:2, laws are being given by God to those individuals, "*either men or women, who desire to take a special vow of a Nazirite, setting themselves apart to the Lord in a special way.*" The scripture found in Numbers 6:3 goes on to declare that these Nazirite's, "*Must give up wine and other alcoholic drinks.*" This may be the source that some use as support for not drinking. However, if one is taking the vow as a Nazirite, one must continue reading all of that section of Leviticus and follow the other requirements as well such as not cutting the hair, eating grapes, raisins or anything from the fruit of the grapevine. This scripture is not addressed to all Christians, but only those who voluntarily desire to take the Nazirite vow to please God.

In Luke 1:15, we are being introduced to the birth and arrival of John the Baptist. An angel of the Lord tells Zechariah that his wife shall have a son and he will be great in the eyes of the Lord. The angel goes on to tell Zechariah that the child "*Must never touch wine or hard liquor.*" This is supported by the passage from Mathew we discussed earlier where Jesus acknowledges that John the Baptist did not drink.

We must pause here and try to bring some clarity to this whole discussion about drinking wine and alcoholic beverages. For there are many reading this and already know that drinking wine or other alcoholic beverages is not a sin and wondering why so much time and effort is devoted to this topic. Then there are some who are even more confused because all of their Christian life and walk, they have been taught that drinking wine and alcoholic beverages were a sin. Thus the reason to expand this discussion because if these scriptures are in the Bible, why is there so much confusion and debate over whether or not a believer/saved Mature Christian can or cannot drink alcoholic beverages?

This is a good place to talk about religious denominations. There are many different denominations, and they each have their own set of beliefs as it relates primarily to drinking alcoholic beverages. Denominational variances, not biblical scripture, have also caused intense infighting among the Christian body on many topics. This has caused Christians of one particular denomination to question another denomination's beliefs since everyone believes that their denomination has gotten the teachings directly from the Bible. If this is true, how can one of these denominations come away with contrast interpretations of the sacred writ?

That is, how can some denominations believe it is okay for their members and pastoral leadership to drink while others explicitly teach against drinking? Remember, we are talking about denominational differences and not biblical scripture. Denominations were created by man and scripture was inspired by God. We find in Second Timothy 3:16-17 these words: *"All scripture is inspired by God and is useful to teach us what is true and to make us realize what is wrong in our lives. It straightens us out and teaches us to do what is right. It is God's way of preparing us in every way, fully equipped for every good thing God want us to do."*

There are no denominations in the Bible. That is why you might find those of the Catholic denomination who drink, but not those of the Baptist denomination. You may find Episcopalians who drink; but not Holiness or Church of God denominations. These are man-made beliefs unique to a particular denomination; not necessarily a requirement of God. While man may believe and have incorporated into his denominational formation a standard that includes members of its denomination not drinking wine or other alcoholic drink; sacred writings, however, has no scripture that supports or identifies a particular denomination nor a prohibition to drinking wine or other alcoholic drink.

Although we happen to be discussing alcohol consumption at present, this is a perfect spot to suggest that before anyone joins a church, they need to know what the church's traditional denominational beliefs are and if the church is practicing those particular beliefs. As a child coming up in the old-fashioned Baptist church, I remember every first Sunday before we took communion, (isn't this an oxymoron) we had to read aloud, in unison, the church's Baptist covenant. In the covenant, it said that as a member of the Baptist church, we would "Refrain from the sale and use of alcohol as an intoxicating beverage." Therefore, if you are a member of a conventional Baptist church or any other denomination that has as a part of its covenant the refraining from the sale and use of alcohol as an intoxicating beverage, then, that may be the reason why the leadership teaches that it is wrong to drink and require members not to drink (but Baptist can drink wine every first Sunday). Remember, it is a covenant and covenants are binding. These covenants are not biblical requirements of salvation or a Godly lifestyle, but strictly a man-made mandate by a particular denomination. Denominations, however, in order to keep confusion over what is a sin or not a sin, should be clear in their teachings the reason or rationale behind their belief or stance on a particular issue. Condemning another denomination as sinful because they believe a man-made denominational tradition, rather than the strict Word of God, is part of the problem within the body of Christ.

As I have shared, I have honored the wishes of my husband because he does not drink alcohol of any kind. He is a man of principle. He teaches what he believes and what he lives. The problem I have is with pastors who preach you should not drink; yet, they drink behind closed doors. I am a firm believer that you should live what you preach. If you drink, then at least don't preach to others that they should not drink. Leave the subject alone. I also feel the same way about pastors who preach to their partners to tithe; yet they do not tithe themselves. Tithing is another topic that I cover in my book, *The MisEducation of The Christian, God's Original Plan for our Finances*. God cannot be pleased with this behavior. Years ago when I was operating my CPA practice; I did a lot of work for churches and their associations. I was newly married and just beginning to see the back office of church leadership. I was asked by a pastor to work with a well-known conference association that was attended by nationally recognized pastors. At the conclusion of the meeting, as usual, all the pastors eat a meal. I was invited to eat at the restaurant with them by the pastor who had asked me to assist with the conference. When the waiter came to take our order, it was evident that this was a place that these particular pastors frequently visited as the server knew them by name and had asked, "Everyone want their usual drink orders?" A pastor that I knew, only from his prominence, grabbed the waiter's hand as if to say, 'Hold on a minute,' and looked to the pastor who had invited me with a questioning glare. The pastor that invited me said, "Oh, it's okay, she's a pastor's wife...she knows how we do." The well-known pastor then smiled and turned to the waiter and said, "Yes, we will take our regular orders." The regular orders proved to be alcoholic beverages. While you already know that I do not believe it is a sin to drink and I had no problem with the fact that they were drinking the alcoholic beverages, but I had an issue with the reality that we as pastors can't come out of our closets on this subject. The Holy writ does not say you cannot drink; therefore, it is incumbent that we pastors help our partners to understand the difference between social drinking and being drunk. Be open and honest with your partners if you do drink and reassure them that you drink responsibly. I know this is a big pill to swallow for pastors of some denominations long entrenched in tradition. The reality is to do anything less is what is causing some divisions within the body of Christ.

The truth of the matter is there are some pastors of some denominations that drink while others insist the opposite is true and that you should not drink wine or liquor of any kind.

So, with all that has been written on this topic we come down to this simple question: "Is it a sin to drink wine and other alcoholic beverages?" The answer is the same as the question about eating. Colossians 2:16 states, *"So don't let anyone condemn you for what you eat or drink, or for not celebrating certain holy days or new-moon ceremonies or Sabbaths."* Verses 20-23 continue with, *"So why do you keep on following rules of the world, such as, 'Don't handle, don't eat, don't touch.' Such rules are mere human teaching about things that are gone as soon as we use them. These rules may seem wise because they require strong devotion, humility, and severe bodily discipline. But they have no effect when it comes to conquering a person's evil thoughts and desires."*

Perhaps this scripture puts a greater perspective about where Christians get a lot of their do's and don'ts. Somewhere along the way we have been taught that Christians must lead a strong, disciplined life in order to be pleasing to God. That is possibly quite accurate; however, the real question is a strong, disciplined life as it relates to what? I argue that the discipline God desires from us is in our study of His Word, in our obedience to His commands, and in our faith that He has everything under control as it relates to our lives. Remember, the scripture First Samuel 15:22 tells us, "*Obedience is far better than sacrifice.*" So if God is not demanding our sacrifice of *fun* what makes us think it is pleasing to Him for us to do so?

Galatians 4:10-11, "*You are trying to find favor with God by what you do or don't do on certain days or months or seasons or years. I fear for you. I am afraid that all my hard work for you was worth nothing.*"

It is so evident, the Apostle Paul in the book of Galatians is trying to tell us that we cannot please God by what we do or don't do because of religious protocol. What we do or don't do must be because God says to do this or don't do this. Paul is genuinely concerned in this passage that Christians are missing the main point of all the preaching and teaching that he has been doing. He is concerned that people believe that doing or not doing things that God has not asked of us will cause God to show special favor on them. This is just not the case. In fact, in Mathew 7:21-23 we find the evidence to support this farce. "*Not all people who sound religious are really godly. They may refer to me as 'Lord,' but they still won't enter the Kingdom of Heaven. The decisive issue is whether they obey my Father in heaven. On judgment day many will tell me,*"

'Lord, Lord, we prophesied in your name and cast out demons in your name and performed many miracles in your name.' But I will reply, 'I never knew you. Go away; the things you did were unauthorized."

God will show favor on those whom he chooses to show favor upon (Romans 9:16); not because of anything we have said or done.

❖ ❖ Prayer ❖ ❖

God, we continually call on You for Your help, guidance and wisdom. There are so many man-made traditions and religions that have permeated the churches and clouded the simple message of loving You, having a relationship with You, accepting Your gift of salvation, and allowing our lives to show that we belong to You. Help our denominational leaders to come together and stop allowing man-made traditions to separate us from the ability to cooperate in the unity of the faith for the furtherance of Your kingdom here on Earth. Help our church leaders not to be afraid to break from man-made traditions and teach and preach the entire Bible from Genesis to Revelation as it is recorded in the Word and not as man has translated it through the years. Help our leaders to have a thirst for revelation in these areas that have been taboo. Give them boldness to stand and preach the gospel and live the gospel that they preach. In the name of Jesus, we pray, AMEN.

❖

CHAPTER NINE

Dancing, Cards, Billiards & Games
Can You Play?

I f God did not want Christians to enjoy life, why then did God instruct the people to have so many festivals honoring Him that required food, drink, and dance? In fact, John 10:10 declares, *"I came that they may have and enjoy life."* (Amplified Bible)

The entire books of Leviticus, Numbers, and Deuteronomy, outline various festivals, holidays, and celebrations that require food and drink. God could have easily instructed us that during these times, we must simply fast and pray only. Yet he did not, and we know God is infallible, and He specifically gave us the Holy Word that contains all answers to every situation we could imagine. Why didn't God instruct Moses to tell us, "Do not drink, feast, or dance?"

We can find many passages in the 66 books where people danced. In Exodus 15:20 we find these words, *"Then Miriam, the prophet, Aaron's sister, took a tambourine and led all the women in rhythm and dance."* This happened because the women wanted to show God how thankful they were for rescuing them from the

Egyptians and safely taking them across the Red Sea. Second Samuel 6:16 is often quoted as the scripture to support dancing. We find King David, the most beloved of all God's men, dancing before the Lord as the Ark of the Covenant is being brought back into the city of Jerusalem.

So, what's the problem with dancing? There is no problem with dancing. It is how we dance that may be inappropriate, not the act of dancing itself. For nowhere in scripture does it specifically say that Christians cannot dance. Again, we do need to be sensitive to how we dance. Remember, we should dance the same way we would dance if Jesus were in attendance. Isn't God present everywhere? God sees all and knows all. Is Jesus holding up the wall at the wedding feast in Canaan; or is Jesus dancing with the other guests and enjoying himself? Remember, Mathew 11:18-19, where Jesus said he *drank and feasted*. So why should it matter where we are if it is God we are ultimately trying to please?

Need anything bear repeating at this point? Where do we get all these do's and don'ts we believe as Christians? Please don't say it is because games did not exist during the Bible days. That's as bad as saying the wine was different during the biblical days than now; so it was okay to drink wine then but not now? The wine may have been different; but there was wine, or some alcoholic beverage, that made people drunk. We just pointed out that Noah got drunk off of something. Even in Acts 2:1-15, when the Holy Spirit fell on the disciples they began to speak in many different languages which confused the people who were viewing them. The people looking did not understand them speaking in the different languages, and so they thought the disciples were drunk. Peter made it clear to those who were watching that they were not drunk. So we can believe that there was, even during those biblical times, some types of games (or wine, or alcoholic drink) that God could have very easily said was inappropriate and forbidden. However, he did not.

Based on everything we have read from the Bible thus far, is there anywhere in the Bible that says we cannot play games? The reality once again is that Christians have refrained from playing games like spades, bid whiz, billiards and, etc. because the world has taken these games and created an environment around them that is not Christian-friendly. So in our efforts as Christians to show the world that we are different and in accordance with the fourteenth chapter of the book of Romans, we convinced ourselves that playing these games were sinful. In other words, most of our recollection about any of these games have centered on gambling, smoking, cursing and drinking to excess. It was not the games themselves that were sinful; it was the individual(s) who brought their vices with them. There is nothing wrong with Christian brothers and sisters coming together to have fun playing games where the environment is conducive to a wholesome family event. In fact, this is probably the biggest trick of Satan. Everyone needs an entertainment outlet. If Satan can convince us that having fun is not an appropriate Christian behavior, then, imagine how many people he can keep away from Christ. Most people don't want to be a hypocrite doing one thing when around close family and friends but never in a million years doing that same thing around their pastor or Christian friends. The Christian church has left those in the pews, Sunday after Sunday, no options by avoiding having important discussions on these topics and offering only a biblical-based answer without practical application. For the Mature Christian in a church that preaches against participating in these activities, they simply keep quiet and dare not tell their Christian friends or their Pastor that they do in fact participate in such activities for fear of being shunned or excluded from participating in leadership roles. For the Unbeliever who is trying to decide whether to accept Jesus Christ into their lives, they choose in many cases to stay in the world and not accept Jesus Christ so they can still have some fun. For the Immature Christian, they are just lost. They don't know which way to turn...indulge or not indulge. It is not the dice, the dancing, the cards, or the pool table that is evil. It is what we do and how we do what we do. This is very much like money. Some churches teach money is evil, and those of significant wealth must have obtained it through ill-gotten ways. My book, *The MisEducation of the Christian, God's Original Plan for our Finances* is a must read. For in it, I discuss that money in and of it self is not evil. It is the love of money and what we will do to get that money, that is evil (First Timothy 6:10). The same is true here. How we dance, (provocative), how we use dice and play cards (gambling), and in what type of environment are the deciding factors.

If Jesus were here on Earth with you, would you invite Him to go along with you for your night out? If you hesitated or your answer is no, then you have answered for yourself that you should not be indulging in that particular behavior.

Jesus had fun, and He wants us to have a good time so go ahead and set aside a family game night. You will be amazed at how much ministry can go forth when brothers and sisters come together and have fun. You will be pleasantly surprised at how much you can learn about what's going on in your children's lives when you spend time with them playing games. Remember, it is the environment that is most important. Remember, Jesus is right there with you. He sees all and knows all.

❖ ❖   Prayer   ❖ ❖

God, You are a God that sent Your Son so that we may have life and have it more abundantly. You believe in the family so much so that You use the family as an example throughout the Bible. Life is supposed to be enjoyable. Help us to know that it is okay to have fun. It's okay to laugh, play games and play with cards. Help us to understand that it is the environment in which we may play these games and the things we may do during these moments that may make it not pleasing to You. Help us to know when the atmosphere of our environment changes. And Lord, help us to avoid participation in any activity in which we would not invite our pastors to go along with us or more importantly would not invite You along if You were still here walking the Earth.
In the name of Jesus, we pray, AMEN.

❖

CHAPTER TEN

Is It Okay To Have Tattoos?

N ow, before you and I begin to talk about tattoos, please know that my assignment is not to judge anybody who may or may not have tattoos. Wherever we fall on this topic, my intent is to provide revelation as given to me to share. The primary focus of this entire book has been to open the dialogue on controversial topics within the body of Christ, and to help enable us to receive the revelations we need to have a solid biblical base for why we do or won't do a particular behavior or activity.

"In the same way, some think one day is more holy than another day, while others think every day is alike. You should each be fully convinced that whichever day you choose is acceptable. Those who worship the Lord on a special day do it to honor him. Those who eat any kind of food do so to honor the Lord since they give thanks to God before eating. And those who refuse to eat certain foods also want to please the Lord and give thanks to God. For we don't live for ourselves or die for ourselves. If we live, it's to honor the Lord. And if we die, it's to honor the Lord. So whether we live or die, we belong to the Lord. Christ died and rose again for

this very purpose—to be Lord both of the living and of the dead. So why do you condemn another believer? Why do you look down on another believer? Remember, we will all stand before the judgment seat of God." (Romans 14:5-10)

Paul starts off this passage of scripture by giving us a good example of two religions who both believe they are correct as it relates to the right day to worship God, although they each worship on different days. Some believe the Sabbath day is Saturday and some believe the Sabbath Day to worship is Sunday. The Seventh Day Adventist think they are correct with Saturday worship and that Baptist or those who worship on Sunday are going to Hell. Those of us that worship on Sunday, think the Seventh Day Adventists are going to Hell. Who is right or are all of us wrong? What Paul is trying to show us is, "Why argue over a day of the week? We need to be convinced in our heart that we worship on the day that God called us to worship." If our heart is right, it doesn't matter whether we're doing it on a Saturday or a Sunday. Paul says if we believe we're supposed to worship on Saturday, don't feel guilty because of a conviction in our spirit that God has told us that the Sabbath is Saturday. But, likewise, if someone is convinced that Sunday is the New Sabbath don't try to condemn or convince them that they are wrong. God isn't really concerned about which day we worship Him as long as we have a Sabbath day of worship. When we get to heaven, there will be no Saturday Christians and Sunday Christians there. Every day will be the Sabbath, worshipping God day and night.

Here is a good place to remind you of our conversation about Unbelievers, Immature and Mature Christians. The purpose of these discussions is not for you to have ammunition for the barbershop gossip. So, please don't go in the barbershop Saturday with a crowd of Unbelievers, and you and some other Christian's start arguing over whether it is okay or not okay to drink, play cards, or have tattoos. There could be a person there who needs to meet Jesus, but because of your public disagreements decides he's not going to anyone's church. Once again, Christians can't seem to agree on what the Bible says so why should that person bother to join the Body of Christ?

Let me be direct: Don't tear apart the work of God over tattoos. That's what the Apostle Paul is saying in Romans 14:20-22, *"Remember, all foods are acceptable, but it is wrong to eat something that makes another person stumble. It is better not to eat meat or drink wine or do anything else if it might cause another believer to stumble. You may believe there's nothing wrong with what you are doing, but keep it between yourself and God. Blessed are those who don't feel guilty for doing something they have decided is right."* It is your responsibility to talk to God, and let God convict you. Don't argue with somebody who says this or says that. Your relationship with Christ is personal and will always be personal.

"To what can I compare this generation? It is like children playing a game in the public square. They complain to their friends, 'We played wedding songs, and you didn't dance, so we played [sad music] – we played funeral songs, but you [wouldn't get sad]." (Matthew 11:16-17)

You know what Jesus is actually saying? You can't win! Jesus says, *"If I play happy music, you're mad because I play happy music. If I play sad music, you don't respond to sad music."* So what is a person suppose to do?

I used all of this as an introduction to tattoos. If I say you can have tattoos, somebody's going to be mad. If I say you can't have tattoos, some will be mad. So I'm just going to share with you what God has given me to share, and let you, as I have done throughout this book, process it for yourself.

Chapter 11 verses 18-19 of the book of Mathew (which we have shared earlier) we see these words which help us to begin this discussion. *"For John didn't spend his time eating and drinking, and you say, 'He's possessed by a demon.' The Son of Man, on the other hand, feasts and drinks, and you say, 'He's a glutton and a drunkard, and a friend of tax collectors and other sinners!' But wisdom is shown to be right by its results."*

Years ago, a local pastor preached the sermon entitled, "If it Ain't One Thing, It's Another." He said, "If I buy a new car, I'm too extravagant. If I don't get a new car, I'm too cheap." He went on to say, "If my wife buys a new dress, we spend too much money. If she doesn't get a new dress, I don't treat her right. If it ain't one thing, it's another. If I try to pastor the church, I'm a dictator... If I don't try to pastor, I don't have any vision. If it ain't one thing ... it's another."

Jesus says the same. No matter what some Christians do, whether they have tattoos or not, whether they drink wine or not, whether they dance or not, play games or not, someone is going to have something to say. You cannot win either way when discussing these topics.

Now, do you understand? These topics are taboo in most churches because the church is afraid to talk about them. There are so many denominational differences of opinions of what Christians can and cannot do. However, people perish for lack of knowledge. It is time for the Body of Christ to once and for all approach these topics from a biblical stance and not a denominational belief. We must do so in order to continue to edify the Saints into Mature Christians who are not hypocrites or just totally confused as they interact with others from another denominational belief.

"Do not trim off the hair on your temples or trim your beards. Do not cut your bodies for the dead, and do not mark your skin with tattoos. I am the Lord. Do not defile your daughter by making her a prostitute, or the land will be filled with prostitution and wickedness. Keep my Sabbath days of rest, and show reverence toward my sanctuary. I am the Lord." (Leviticus 19:27-30)

This is typically the first scripture read when talking about tattoos not being pleasing to God. However, the first thing people will say is, "Well, that's under the law. We don't live under the law anymore." However, Jesus has a response to everyone who uses this argument whether for tattoos, tithing, or any other Old Testament topic.

Mathew 5:17-18 we find Jesus sharing these words: *"Don't misunderstand why I have come. I did not come to abolish the law of Moses or the writings of the prophets. No, I came to accomplish their purpose. I tell you the truth until Heaven and Earth disappear, not even the smallest detail of God's law will disappear until its purpose is achieved."*

Too many Christians, although they will read these same scriptures will still follow up any such conversation with Galatians 3:23-25. Read what Galatians declares: *"Before the way of faith in Christ was available to us, we were placed under guard by the law. We were kept in protective custody, so to speak, until the way of faith was revealed. Let me put it another way. The law was our guardian until Christ came ...it protected us until we could be made right with God through faith. And now that the way of faith has come, we no longer need the law as our guardian."*

We need to look closely at this scripture. It does not say we no longer needed the law; it said we no longer needed the law as a guardian. But the Law still exists. The Law is no longer needed as a means of our salvation. Romans 10:9 is our means of salvation, and we have already spent a considerable amount of effort to help us understand salvation and how to receive it.

Listen to the language; he says the law was a guardian. A guardian is only needed for children. A guardian is for the Immature believer. What Christ is saying is, when you're Immature, you don't know right from wrong, and therefore you need a guardian to guide and teach you right from wrong. Hence the Law was given. He said, *"I hope you mature to the point, one day, that you don't need a guardian anymore."* Most will agree, that once mature, you continue to do what you were taught or even if you don't, you know that you are not doing what you were taught. In the United States, you are considered a legal adult when you turn twenty-one; you don't need a guardian anymore; you can make your own decisions.

"Well then, am I suggesting that the law of God is sinful? Of course not! In fact, it was the law that showed me my sin. I would never have known that coveting is wrong if the law had not said, "You must not covet." But sin used this command to arouse all kinds of covetous desires within me! If there were no law, sin would not have that power. At one time I lived without understanding the law. But when I learned the command not to covet, for instance, the power of sin came to life." (Romans 7:7-9)

Because of the law, one knows what is right and wrong. How would we know what sin is if the law was never given? People would be walking around shooting everybody if the Law did not say, *"Thou shall not kill* (Exodus 20:13)." That's why Jesus had to come to fulfill the Law and allow us to be saved by His ultimate sacrifice of His life. The law was showing us what is pleasing to God and what we should and should not be doing.

Let me make one final point before we continue on the Law and the Old Testament. Far too often, some Christians will say we only have to follow and read the New Testament, however, the Bible contains both the Old and New Testament. To fully understand the New Testament, one must read the Old Testament. Our Ten Commandments are written in the Old Testament, and very few would doubt or question that we must still follow the Ten Commandments.

Here is another way of looking at the Law. If we can get rid of the law, why don't we tell the state of Virginia (or any state), "Take away all the speed limit signs?" But if they did that how would we know when we were speeding? Some might like driving at a hundred miles per hour while others prefer sixty miles per hour. With no law, everyone would drive at whatever speed they desired, and we know that would not be good. So, the law is, so everyone knows what acceptable and unacceptable behavior is.

It is amazing to see how Christians have come to interpret scripture or not even use scripture at all to justify their actions. Unfortunately, most Christians, along with the secular world, rather than using scripture as the foundation of their decision-making, base their behavior on how they have been cultured. So, tattooing, now, has become so popular, that culturing has told us it's acceptable. That's why Romans 12:2 exists. It says, *"Don't copy the behavior and customs of this world, but let God transform you into a new person by changing the way you think."* If we keep watching the world, the world will convince us to do things that are not what God would desire for us to do.

Isaiah 44:5, *"Some will proudly claim, 'I belong to the Lord. Others will say, 'I am a descendant of Jacob, Some will write the Lord's name on their hands."*

Here is a scripture that some have been using to say it is okay to get a tattoo because this scripture says, *"Some will write the Lord's name on their hands."* However, we must understand that Isaiah was an "Eschatological prophet." That means, he prophesied about stuff that had not happened yet. That's why Isaiah could tell us that there will come a *Savior; His Name shall be called Wonderful Counselor, Prince of Peace; the government shall be upon His shoulder, and to His reign, there shall come no end.* Nobody else thought Isaiah knew what he was talking about...until Mary got pregnant. Mary doesn't even understand, so Gabriel had to come to her and remind her that Isaiah prophesied this four hundred years ago. (Luke 1:26-38)

Isaiah is not talking about right now. He is talking about the end times. All Christians have been taught in the Body of Christ about the mark of the beast. However, few have been taught that there is going to be a mark put on the believer as well.

Everybody during the Tribulation is going to have a mark. It's just that some people will have a mark on their forehead that's going to be 666, (Revelation 13:16) and some people are going to have the mark of God on their foreheads. (Revelation 7:3)

There's an Old Testament Biblical motif for this. When the Israelites got ready to come out of Egypt, God tells them in Exodus 12:13, *"But the blood on your doorposts will serve as a sign, marking the houses where are staying. When I see the blood, I will pass over you. This plague of death will not touch you."*

So the same applies during the Tribulation. The only way the death angel is going to know who not to kill and condemn is that he's going to have to look at the heads or hands for the mark of the believer among the people that are living through the Tribulation. When the Death Angel sees the seal of God, he is going to pass by them. However, when he sees the Mark of the Beast (or 666), the Death Angel will seal their fate.

"He required everyone—small and great, rich and poor, free and slave—to be given a mark on the right hand or on the forehead. And no one could buy or sell anything without that mark, which was either the name of the beast or the number representing his name." (Revelation 13:16-17)

This is Satan, the antichrist, who will be reigning during the time of the Millennium – what we call the period of Tribulation. When we read Revelation, it is clear that the world is going to become divided and everyone will have to declare whether or not they are a follower of

Christ. Followers of Christ will have a seal of God placed on their head. Those not accepting the seal of Satan, the Bible says, *"Will not be able to buy and sell."* So, the pressure of the Tribulation is the challenge of being able to buy food and supplies needed for survival unless 666 is on your head or hand.

Now, to bring closure to the topic of whether Christians should be tattooing their body here is the bottom line. As a follower of God, He is going to mark us. As a follower of Satan, they too will have a mark. Well, then, the mark must be about ownership. The mark or tattoo shows to whom we belong. So, if we have tattoos, then we must think we own ourselves. However, from all the scripture we have found the only person that is supposed to write on the [body] is Jehovah, if we are followers of Christ.

"Don't you realize that all of you together are the temple of God and that the Spirit of God lives in you? God will destroy anyone who destroys this temple. For God's temple is holy, and you are that temple." (1 Corinthians 3:16-17)

"Don't you realize that your body is the temple of the Holy Spirit, who lives in you and was given to you by God? You do not belong to yourself, for God bought you with a high price. So you must honor God with your body." (1 Corinthians 6:19-20)

Our body is the Temple of the Holy Spirit. How many people, if given a white canister of spray paint, would go to their church, which is the temple of the Lord and write something on the outside of the building? Most would say, "I would dare not write on the temple of the Lord." Then, what is the difference between the temple (building) and the temple (body)? Our body is the temple of God! So how can we let someone take a tattoo gun and write something on our body? Why are we doing it to the temple of God that is our body if we wouldn't do it to the temple of God that is our church?

So what can I say to those of you who may already have tattoos? First, I pray that you also pray to God and seek his guidance on what to do, if anything, about your tattoo. I am on the side of no tattoos. Does that mean having a tattoo will send you to Hell? No, I don't believe so. While it may be displeasing to God that you have written on your body, I do not believe it is a sin unto death. I believe that if you pray to God, He will give you a conviction about whether you should or should not have your tattoo. I know there are some who have already had their tattoos surgically removed. Some just cover up their tattoos. Others are still proudly displaying their tattoos. If you happen to have tattoos and after praying to God you are convicted that you should not have tattoos, remember God is a forgiving God. It is what you do after you receive revelation about what is right or what is wrong that counts. If God convicts you that you should not have tattoos, don't say, "Well I already got tattoos, so I may as well get more." No, that is the devil trying to trick you. Stop getting tattoos. The old tattoos, like any other displeasing activity, will be covered by the grace of God knowing your heart to seek Him out.

❖ ❖   Prayer   ❖ ❖

God hear my prayer, search my heart, and know that I really
want to hear directly from You. I may have gotten my tattoo
for various reasons. I may even have a Christian symbol
tattoo but I need to know from You how You feel
about my tattoos. Direct my steps as it relates
to the disposition of my tattoos.
In the Name of Jesus, I pray, AMEN.

❖❖ CONCLUSION ❖❖

E arlier in our discussion, we defined an Unbeliever, an Immature Christian, and a Mature Christian. It was important to define these terms because we needed to understand the interdependence each has with the other and the role each plays in our decisions on what we can and cannot do. Paul, in First Corinthians 8:1-13 says, that Mature Christians may have the knowledge that certain things are okay to do and eat. But that knowledge is of no value if the love of God is not being displayed in our interaction with the Immature Christians. It goes on to say that Mature Christians must be careful with their knowledge and freedom because they will be held accountable for causing a weaker Christian to stumble because of their actions. Paul says even though we know it is alright to do a particular thing, yet a weaker Christian who believes it is wrong to do what we are doing sees us; then we might encourage the weaker Christian to do something that he believes is wrong. We already know, from previous scripture, that if someone does something they believe is wrong, then it is a sin (Romans 14:23). Paul concludes with, therefore, that he will never eat meat again if it causes another brother to stumble in their faith. Paul also says in Romans 15:1, *"We may know that these things make no difference, but we cannot just go ahead and do them to please ourselves. We must be considerate of the doubts and fears of those who think these things are wrong."*

Does all this sound like I have been vacillating? Were you looking for a straight yes or no answer to all of your questions about what you can and cannot do if you call yourself a Mature Christian? I pray that you do not feel as if a straight answer has not been given but that you have a sound, biblical foundation for whatever decision you make regarding the issues discussed. The bottom line is that all matters such as drinking, playing cards, dancing, getting tattoos, and many, many others can all be summed up and responded to using Second Corinthians 6:3-4 where it says, *"We try to live in such a way that no one will be hindered from finding the Lord by the way we act, and so no one can find fault with our ministry. In everything we do, we try to show that we are true ministers of God."*

As I started to research and seek God's face in this area of ministry, I knew these would be difficult subject matters to undertake. I have been laboring, studying, and seeking God in this work for many years. Everyone will not agree with all that has been shared. That's okay. I know everyone is responsible for what they do or don't do and will have to give an individual account to God. My prayer is that I am not misleading, or misdirecting any

Unbeliever or Immature Christian in the information shared in this book. I count myself among the mature saints, being called into the ministry specifically to teach practical life applications from the biblical perspective. I pray consistently for new revelation that will encourage and strengthen other Christians to continue and grow in their faith walk. To that end, I give all glory to God for the inspiration and courage to bring to life through this book an emancipating revelation on issues that have too long been swept under the rugs and ineffectively dealt with in the Christian community.

May God add a blessing to these words so that they may be received with the purest of intention and bless the hearts of those who would have an ear to hear.

Amen.

❖❖ PASTORAL COMMENTS ❖❖
Workshop Questions & Answers

The discussion and teachings in this book, *You Can't Do What? The Real Meaning of Your Salvation* was initially introduced during a particular teaching moment at Mt. Lebanon Missionary Baptist Church, in Chesapeake, Virginia. The discussion was led by the author, Elder Dr. Valerie K. Brown, and the question and answer session was led by her husband, and then senior pastor of the church, Rev. Dr. Kim Walter Brown.

We thought it would be beneficial to our readers to include the questions and discussion that followed the teachings you have just read.

Pastoral opening comments

"I was scared of tonight. I had been wrestling with releasing Elder Valerie to teach on this topic. I was scared, not of the contents that were to be taught; but of how people would perceive and possibly misinterpret what was taught. The reality is, however, that these are topics, like many others, whose time has come for the church to be open to discussing. Churches are afraid to tackle the tough issues and just as Elder Valerie has already articulated, many Christians are suffering because they don't know the answers to many such questions about the lifestyle a Christian should be exemplifying."

"Let me just say for the record before we even begin to answer questions, that I do not drink wine or alcoholic beverages. Elder Valerie testified to you that I requested that she not drink once we became engaged to be married. God gave me a new revelation with respect to Joshua and his statement, 'As for me and my house.' I agree that I cannot literally go to the Bible and find a passage that says you should not drink. I can find passages that say you should not get drunk. What I found out, however, is that our young people are not like we were when we were young. They do not simply accept what we say. If I tell young people that the Bible says do not drink, they ask for the scripture. When you are not able to give them a scripture that specifically says, 'do not drink (dance or any other topic we have discussed throughout this book) because it is a sin,' they begin to question what else are you telling them they can't do because the Bible says so when you can't find it in the Bible. It is time we stop being hypocritical and simply tell the truth. For those gray areas, simply say, the Bible may not literally say thus and so, but as for me and my house and for how the Holy Spirit has convicted me, I believe it is wrong to drink alcoholic beverages."

"It is time for each of us to become Mature Christians and seek God's guidance on our lives. Everyone wants the preacher to simply tell you, yes or no, as it relates to certain behaviors that they can or can't do. You must seek God for yourself. God will answer you."

"Unfortunately, Christians give more respect to their pastors than they do to God. I was attending a wedding reception recently and the photographer was standing outside smoking a cigarette. However, when I approached the photographer, he quickly put the cigarette behind his back so I could not see that he was smoking. Well the smoke was rising from behind his head, and you know you can smell smoke a mile away. I wanted to tell the photographer, 'Don't hide the cigarette from me, God can see the cigarette. In fact, if you don't move that cigarette, you will likely burn a hole in that tuxedo you just rented and will be paying for it.' Why are we so hypocritical? We have no problem with a person smoking a pipe or cigar, yet we will judge a person smoking a cigarette. What's the difference? Both contain tobacco. It's time church folks acknowledge that church-going people have the most dysfunctional rationale on what Christians can and cannot do. Even with their strict man-made laws of dos and don'ts, (which are somehow suppose to make you holier) statistics show Christians (especially preachers) have the highest divorce rates and most dysfunctional families. This simply does not add up."

"Most of us have the testimony that as children we were dragged to church by our parents. But when we grew up we stopped coming to church so that we could have 'some fun.' We went out into the world and after we were tired of having our fun, we came back to the church. Where are we getting the theology that being in the church means you can't have fun? I believe it is because we have such a high Christology. That is, our Jesus would never have fun. We believe that while Jesus was at the wedding feast, (before he changed the water into wine), the D.J. played only gospel music and no one danced. But when Jesus left, the D.J. changed his music to the secular music of the day and 'the party began.' Does that sound familiar? That is exactly what Christians do today. While the pastor is at the reception, only gospel music is played. As soon as the pastor leaves, the D.J. gets the signal that it is now okay to bring out the rap music and the alcoholic beverages. Why do you have receptions in locations with dance floors and bars, if you have no intention of dancing or drinking?"

"Please understand, that Pastor Brown, Elder Brown, nor Mt. Lebanon Missionary Baptist Church, taught you here tonight that it is okay to drink, dance, play cards, etc. What we taught you is that the Bible does not literally say you cannot do these things. Each of you must become mature enough to determine for yourself if doing these things is okay for you. I believe if there is anything you would not do in front of me, (Bishop Brown and most importantly in front of Jesus) then you should not being doing it."

Question 1:

"Pastor, I believe it is okay for me to drink, yet I heard you say not to drink if it causes another to stumble. I can even agree not to drink in front of those that I may cause to stumble, so am I okay?"

Pastoral response:

"Let me just use this example for you. As a member of the choir who leads solos, how is drinking potentially hurting your witness? For example, you go into the store to purchase your alcoholic beverages. The cashier engages you in conversation. Then on Sunday, you step forward to sing your song, A M A Z I N G....(My God is Amazing), and you look and see the cashier sitting front row center. What is the cashier thinking? The cashier could be thinking, 'Hey, that's the woman who purchased the wine last night, no wonder she is singing my God is amazing. It's the wine that's singing.' Now the cashier may or may not think this way, but my point is that I am just too afraid of a negative impact on my witness by taking a drink. I constantly ask myself, 'Is that one drink worth losing my witness?' For me, it is not worth it."

Question 2:

"Can you clarify church doctrine and how it varies from church to church and denomination to denomination? At what point is it the responsibility of the church to let people know what they believe or is it more important to get people to accept Christ into their lives?"

Pastoral response:

"Unfortunately, churches take doctrine (created by man) to the Word of God rather than going to the Word of God to get their doctrine. The first thing you need to be sure of is that any church is a bible believing church. No church has gotten everything right yet. I firmly believe every church needs to be an interdenominational church because every denomination has gotten some things right and some things wrong. For example, in the Pentecostal church, the pastor is the leader. He can make decisions. They follow order and authority as described in the Bible. But in the Baptist church, they got ordinances correct, yet in some Baptist churches, the Pastor is nothing more than a missionary. He can make no decisions. These are only examples and we did not come to discuss differences in denominations, however, at Mt. Lebanon we teach what we believe in our new member classes."

"In the first new member class, we teach what we believe and say to potential members that it is okay if you decide after the classes, that you do not want to become a member here. Our church is not for everyone. We would rather you seek another church home (and we will help you find the right location for you) than stay and cause division in our church. The main purpose for the existence of the church is to bring people to Christ. We should not be concerned with the number of members we have; but with the number of people who have accepted Christ into their lives."

Question 3:

"I really appreciate the teachings of tonight. I was even impressed that Elder Valerie felt the liberty to teach in pants tonight. (Laughter) As a minister myself, I constantly feel confined about what I can and cannot do to please others. I understand Romans 14 and the discussion about if it offends my brother or sister, I should refrain. But if that is the case, at what point do you draw the line. There is always going to be someone who is offended. You can spend your whole life worrying about what others think."

Pastoral response:

"Wow, Valerie...you want to take that one? (Pause and Elder shakes her head, No!) You're right. I don't want you to take that one because I know what you are going to say. You don't care what people think. Valerie is delivered from what people think or say about her." (Applause from participants)

Valerie's response:

"I really am delivered from what people say and think about me. It is not, however, that I don't care; in fact I care a lot. Everyone wants people to like them and never say negative things about them. The reality is, unfortunately, that I learned a long time ago, that you can never please everyone. So I have learned how not to be overly concerned or let what people say bother me to that extent. I believe as Second Corinthians instructs that we should live our lives so that our fruit and works speak for themselves. That way, if someone says something negative about us, people will not see those particular negative fruit displayed through our lifestyle. Then those people will be forced to question the truth in those negative comments."

"When we first came to Mt. Lebanon, I was the typical pastor's wife. I sat on the second pew with my big, brim hat on, smiled at everyone, and said nothing at church meetings. Church members were happy. However, as I matured in Christ, I began to change. I remember one church meeting I raised my hand to comment on a topic that was controversial. My husband, the pastor, refused to recognize my hand. Finally, one of the mothers of the church, said, 'Pastor when are you going to call on your wife. Last I know, she joined the church and has a right to speak like any other member.' My husband's response was, "I know, but I also know what she is going to say."

"That was the beginning of my transition. Over the years, I have come to be the person I am now in ministry. There is no pretense. I am no longer trying to be the 'perfect pastor's wife.' I am trying to be who God created me to be. I thank God daily for the church members we now have at Mt. Lebanon. They allow me to be me. That is so important for pastor's wives. Mature Christians and Immature Christians (notice I did not say, 'church members') want real people...not just people who are one thing on Sunday and something else during the week. We have had some members leave since our coming to Mt. Lebanon for whatever reason(s), but we have grown and I believe God has shown favor on Mt. Lebanon because we are truly trying to be obedient to the Word of God and live our lives as examples to others."

Pastoral response:

"The bottom line is you are not going to win regardless of what you do. You will never be able to walk in the anointing of God worrying about what people say. You need to surround yourself with people who are positive influences in your life."

Valerie's added response:

"We have also just proven tonight, that the average Christian is not sure themselves how they should be living so why are you depending on them to tell you how you should be living your life? Everyone will think differently. It will be impossible to satisfy everyone."

Question 4:

"Pastor, I have always been taught that alcohol contained chemicals that affect the brains. I know different people have different tolerance levels but isn't this why people should not drink?"

Pastoral response:

"Yes, different people do have different tolerance levels. In fact, if I drink a thimble full of alcohol, I am affected. You think I am out the box now, you should see me after a drink. In high school, I was crazy after drinking and I cannot afford to lose any brain cells due to drinking.

Some of you may be able to afford to lose some memory cells, but I can't. The Bible does teach that your body is the temple of God. If you believe that then you should guard what goes into your body; including alcohol."

Question 5:

"Pastor, I am taking away from this moment that everyone should simply be for real. I drink and if anyone asks me, I will tell them I drink."

Pastoral response:

"What I find is the church is the most judgmental institution. My job as your pastor is to preach and teach until you reach a point that you are doing what God desires for your life. The reason, perhaps, that you are still a member here is because I have not judged you out of the church because you have acknowledged that you drink. I need church folks to explain to me the difference between a drinker and someone who gossips about the pastor, the church, and the other members until the cows come home. We never judge them. Are you telling me that gossips will be in heaven and drinkers will not?"

Question 6:

"Pastor, I take away from this moment that we should all be striving to be Mature Christians. I liked when Elder Valerie defined the three categories we could be in. As a Mature Christian I need to recognize that how I act and things I do is a process of change. What I do today, I might not do tomorrow. I must recognize that when I first accept Christ, everything will not immediately change; but will change as I grow in maturity."

Pastoral response:

"Add to that the fact that people don't expect their pastor to change and grow. Church people assume that once someone is called into the ministry, they know everything. This is just not true. Pastors are growing as well. Pastors should be coming into new revelations each and every day that they commune with Holy Spirit."

Question 7:

"It's all about spiritual growth for me and not causing another to stumble, however, my comment is directed toward the dancing. I know people are judgmental about our youth and adults dancing in the church. However, for me it is worship and giving praises to God when I dance. For those who don't know me, it was not too long ago that I was in a wheel chair and was unable to dance or even walk. God healed me. So when you see me get up in morning worship and dance, don't judge me critically because you don't know what I have been through. I remember when I could not feel my feet, let alone stand on them to dance unto the Lord. We really need to be careful about how we judge people and their actions."

❖❖ **APPENDIX** ❖❖

The following questions are excellent for determining beliefs about certain experiences we encounter. Answer each query prior to reading this book and record your results. Take the questionnaire again after you have finished reading and compare your answers to see if your opinions/revelation about each topic have changed. This is also a great exercise to stimulate discussion in any small or large group setting.

YOU CAN'T DO WHAT?

Questionnaire for Study Groups

Circle your choices (You may choose more than one)

1. I am saved because:
    a.   I'm a good person
    b.   I have confessed and believe Romans 10:9
    c.   I do good works
    d.   I got baptized

2. Is it wrong to drink wine, beer, and other alcoholic beverages?
    a.   Yes
    b.   No

3. If drinking is wrong, why?
    a.   My parents told me.
    b.   I read it in the Bible.
    c.   I heard a preacher say it was wrong.
    d.   I don't know how I know…that's just what I believe.

4. If I drink am I still saved?
    a.   Yes
    b.   No

5. Is dancing in church wrong?
    a.   Yes
    b.   No

6. If dancing in church is wrong, the reason(s) is:
   a. The church is holy ground.
   b. Church folks will talk about me.
   c. Dance moves are too provocative.
   d. Dancing is not acceptable in my church.
   e. Dancing is for the nightclub only.

7. Is it wrong to dance at social events?
   a. Yes
   b. No

8. If dancing at social events is wrong, why do you feel this way?
   a. I heard a preacher say it was wrong.
   b. Sends the wrong message about Christians.
   c. Dancing is too provocative.
   d. I don't know…I just think it's wrong.

9. Is it okay to play card games such as bid whiz, spades, etc?
   a. Yes
   b. No

10. Christians should not play games with dice such as Monopoly because:
   a. It involves Money.
   b. It's gambling.
   c. We may get addicted.
   d. I don't know…I just think it's wrong.

11. It is okay to eat pork, chitterlings, crabs and other such delicacies?
   a. Yes
   b. No

12. Christians should not eat pork, chitterlings, crabs or such delicacies because:
   a. The Bible says we should only eat certain foods.
   b. Momma said not to.
   c. Those foods are not healthy for Christians to eat.
   d. People use alcoholic beverages to cook a lot of those types of foods.

13. Is it okay to have a tattoo?
   a. Yes
   b. No

14. Having a tattoo is wrong because:
   a. Only sinners have tattoos.
   b. The Bible says so…I think.
   c. I just believe it's wrong.
   d. I don't know.

15. I'm going to Hell if I…
   a. Drink
   b. Dance
   c. Play games with dice
   d. Have a tattoo
   e. Don't accept Jesus Christ as my Personal Savior

❖❖ ABOUT THE AUTHOR ❖❖

Elder Valerie K. Brown is a native of Chesapeake, Virginia. Elder Brown readily serves beside her husband, Bishop Kim Walter Brown, D. Min. The Presiding Prelate of the Mount Global Fellowship of Churches with locations currently in Chesapeake, Virginia; Elizabeth City, NC; Charlotte, NC; and Yorktown, Virginia. Bishop Brown serves as the Senior Site Pastor of the Chesapeake location of Mount Lebanon Missionary Baptist Church. Elder Valerie serves as the Executive Pastor over the Global Fellowship. Together they are the proud parents of two children, James and Kimberly, one daughter-in-law, Keshia, and one grandson, James Emmanuel.

Elder Brown has an earned doctorate in Business Management from The Weatherhead School of Management, Case Western Reserve University in Cleveland, Ohio. Dr. Brown received her CPA certification (inactive) in 1980 in the State of Virginia and had served as an Associate Professor of Management at the Samuel D. Proctor School of Theology at Virginia Union University in Richmond, Virginia where she taught Church Administration, Finance, and Leadership in the Masters of Divinity Program.

Elder Brown is also the author of *"What's In a Title, A New Leadership Paradigm,"* and *"The MisEducation of The Christian, God's Original Plan for our Finances."*